The Church:

Hope of the World

Cardinal John Wright

The Church: Hope of the World

Edited by

Rev. Donald W. Wuerl

PROW BOOKS

8000 - 39th Avenue
Kenosha, Wisconsin 53141

vi

Foreword

One of the aspects of Cardinal Wright's life in Rome is that described once in a syndicated news column as "his refusal to be stuck behind a desk." This, in fact, refers to his preference for pastoral work and people rather than clerical duties and the office. Perhaps the basis for the notoriety of this side of the Cardinal's priestly life is the great deal of travelling that has particularly characterized his stay thus far in Rome. These travels, which usually come under one of three headings: official business (of which we shall say no more), visits and talks to gatherings of priests, and pastoral or speaking engagements all related to his work for the priesthood. This last category is the one that seems at the moment to be expanding—given the Cardinal's ability to relate to priests generally and the timeliness of most of his themes. This apostolate, of carrying words of joy, consolation, hope and faith to others, has on more than one occasion received the personal encouragement of the Pope. Once, in private audience with our Holy Father, the Cardinal asked if he had any particular approach to the solution of the massive problems of the hour facing not only the faithful but all of us men and women whose uniting bond is mere existence. The reply is a classic one. The Holy Father said, "Preach the faith, and then repeat it, repeat it, repeat it." It is obviously the Pope's own formula: *Repeat, Repeat, Repeat!*

Since the Cardinal's arrival in Rome, as the Prefect of the Congregation of the Clergy charged with the overseeing and encouragement of the pastoral life and ministry of the Church's nearly 450,000 priests, he has taken very seriously the injunction to preach the word, "both in season and out of season, when convenient and inconvenient." The list of cities visited, in Italy alone, reads like the highway advertisement for "Pavesi" stands (the local equivalent of Howard Johnson). In less than two years he has visited all the major towns of the Italian peninsula, and most twice, in reply to invitations that he preach or give lectures. This present collection will contain some of the talks that are the cause of such apostolic journeys. Beginning with the town of Passo della Mendola on the Austrian frontier and working our way through Genova, the city of Christopher Columbus, to Florence with its tradition of art and elegance, to Naples, the heart of the Italian southland, and back again to the Eternal City, we will collect various talks which draw their direction and tone from the central theme of this collection—The Church: Hope of the World.

All of these talks occasion many a pastoral visit, sometimes a comic anecdote and always an opening on to the life, thoughts and hearts of huge numbers of the faithful. These believers represent backgrounds as diverse as the 400 German, Dutch and Eastern European priests who met in Munster, Germany, for a conference with the Cardinal, to the crowds gathered at the Shrine of Our Lady of the Rosary in Pompei or those come together at the Cathedral of Capua to celebrate their 1000th anniversary as an Archdiocese. This last named city is in the south of Italy not far from Caserta, now famous for its attempt to secede from the Republic of Italy when its soccer team was dropped from the major leagues. Capua claims to have received the faith from St. Paul himself as he made his way up the coast of Italy to Rome. There lives in Capua an Archbishop who was responsible for our most recent visit to Capua. It seems that a relatively large group of Indian sisters from Kerala (the ones the papers were pleased to refer to as slaves) were studying in his See city. They had come to live in an Italian convent while they undertook studies in various fields from medicine to the growing of a better brand of yield-rich wheat. The Archbishop's problem was simple. The sisters spoke no Italian and declined to learn it, as they were only temporary residents planning to return home. He spoke no English, yet felt it his duty to look after the spiritual and religious life of the sisters in their sojourn in his diocese and wanted to plan a few hours of prayer and renewal. So he turned to the Cardinal, who agreed to spend time preaching to and praying with these sisters. The entire mood of the day was summed up in the delightful farewell that the sisters staged as we prepared to leave. As the Cardinal and the Archbishop came out of the convent to get in the car for the drive home, all the Kerala sisters gathered round the car and, pointing to the Archbishop, wagged their fingers, giggling cheerfully, "You no speak English," as if he alone on the face of the earth had never mastered the tongue.

In any case the visit there for the day of recollection while on the way to Pompei for the address which is contained in this collection, does provide a glimpse into what usually surrounds such travels.

The next largest group of talks are those given by Cardinal Wright in English either in the United States answering invitations to speak during his infrequent visits home or articles written for publication in Europe.

Since the style of the Cardinal is all his own the editor's pen has been used only rarely and then only to eliminate a parochial opening or closing paragraph. The translations are for the most part those of the Cardinal, as he had kindly given them for this publication. In order to keep as much as possible of the original flavor of the talks as they were delivered, the text has been left untouched, so that in some cases the reader finds himself addressed as if he were part of the audience to whom the Cardinal was speaking in the second person. The apology this editor offers is that of his wish to keep the talks as "untouched up" as possible.

The title of the first talk in this collection, "The Church of Promise," sets the theme and tone of the entire book. Given the anxiety and confusion that plagues many in the Church today, the Cardinal sets forth reasons in his talks for both our encouragement and confidence in Christ's on-going life and activity within His Church. With clarity and force some of the mist that clouds the vision of a number of the faithful is dispelled by re-affirming the content of the Church's ancient faith. Rather than rejoice in the pleasant rest that doubt affords, the obvious intent of the author

is to recall to clear vision the challenge that is the firm uncondi-
tioned commitment to Christ that is the stuff of faith.

I have taken the liberty of selecting only those talks or articles
that resolve around the central theme and have divided them in
this manner:

The first few touch on the exciting work that is the call to
teach the faith. With this are some of the problems that have grown
up to hinder the execution of that mission of witness. The emphasis
in this section falls rather heavily on the work of priests — since
they must labor in an extraordinary manner to fulfill Christ's
mandate.

As the special involvement of the priest in social problems of
the day becomes a recurring event it seems helpful to reaffirm the
specific spiritual dimension that these ministers of God's word are
expected to bring to all the works that build up the Kingdom of
God. Following St. Paul's inspiration, "If Christ is not risen then
our faith be in vain," I have placed Cardinal Wright's sermon on
the Resurrection at the head of the section that contains his reflections on justice, peace and the present cultural condition.

This is followed by the final section which touches on the most
maligned tenet of the faith today — the place and primacy of Peter
and his successors within the Church. The collection closes with
the Cardinal's personal anecdotes and recollections on Pope John
XXIII, the Pope so regularly hailed as having ushered in the
present age of the Church of Promise.

DONALD W. WUERL

Contents

Introduction

Father Donald Wuerl, with singular dedication and diligence, has compiled this collection of addresses which I have given, most of them in Italian which he has translated, during the three years that I have served in Rome. My debt to him for work far beyond the call of duty of a personal secretary is obvious and it is pleasant to record it in this brief prefatory note.

The basis of Father Wuerl's selection of conferences has been the way in which the material selected helps manifest the manner in which the Church remains the world's hope. All rhetorical pretentions that other movements or institutions, political or cultural, constitute "the last, best hope of mankind" vanish before the conquering hope that comes from Christ, His Church, His teaching and His servants. They may be natural means and instruments to humane progress and world peace; but without the Spirit of God, which the Church communicates, they are valid, sometimes naturally sound and true but incapable of enduring efficacy.

Large areas of the world may have lost, as it is sometimes asserted by those who have themselves done so, belief in the "credibility" of the Church; the Church remains, nonetheless, the hope of mankind. Faith teaches this; some of these talks indicate that history confirms by experience the teaching of faith.

The conferences and sermons brought together here represent part of the talks given on this central theme in various parts of Italy and, in the case of two of them, the United States. Actually, most of my preaching in Italy and France has been on the saints, convinced as I am that they are the living evidence of the power of God to transform men, the proof of the hope that the faith and charity brought into the world by the Church can continue to produce men and women from among ourselves who demonstrate that the Church is the hope of the world. Visiting for liturgical celebrations the great sanctuaries of St. Joan, St. Thomas Becket and other saints beyond number, I have been profoundly impressed by the contemporary character (what Italians call *attualitá* and what we call by that omnibus word "relevance") of even long dead saints for our times. Unfortunately, one cannot name a single living statesman or politician who is as pertinent to or effective for the problems of the hour as is St. Thomas More. Neither can one look for much hope of Christian victory over the spirit of the world—the spirit at the heart of its problems—as long as we find among us precious few Edmund Campions, Margaret Clitherows, Maximilian Kolbes and *holy* "hippies" such as I take St. Joan, St. Francis of Assisi, St. Roch and St. Joseph Benedict Labre to have been.

These are instances of the Church at work through men and women as the hope of the world. It would be helpful, perhaps, to put together in a future book some of the sermons we have preached in the towns that produced these saints and the sanctuaries which recall them. Meanwhile, the present book is largely a recollection of principles to which these saintly persons gave life and persuasive example. Those who profit from it should be grateful to its editor, Father Wuerl, and may be disposed, please God, to pray for the undersigned.

✠ JOHN CARDINAL WRIGHT

VATICAN CITY
EASTER, 1972

I
The Church of Promise

I think it fair to say that the mood within the Church today is one of apprehension. I suppose a more accurate, certainly more spiritual word to use in describing that mood, would be to call it a mood of solicitude. This puts us in the tradition of Saint Paul who, confronted with the problems which vexed or threatened the early apostolic Church, confessed that he felt profoundly moved by a solicitude for the Church as a whole in its every part.

Such is our mood today. We meet, all of us, in small groups for conversation, in large groups for policy-making conventions dominated by a solicitude sometimes too anxious to articulate. Sometimes we are so tormented that we articulate, either in our speeches or our resolutions, with exaggeration or with excessive passion, the kind of defeatism and emotional discouragement which is the caricature of solicitude, indeed not solicitude at all, but anxiety run ragged.

I sense this mood in Catholics who love the Church and are concerned with its relation to the world, including the image it projects and the influence it exercises within the world. It is healthy in so far as it reveals a love for the Church and a proper pre-occupation with the problems of the times. It is unhealthy in that it can undermine the faith, diminish joy in that faith and increase the sense of frustration which is the father of confusion and renders you impotent to help the Church you love so much. That mood is undoubtedly intensified by some of the sad, not to say scandalous events reported in the papers you read every day, hear whispered about by your children, carry in your minds as you go about your work and inevitably find creeping into your conversations, particularly those about the state of the Church.

Accordingly I think it wise to meet this mood head on. First of all let me underscore that the present mood of solicitude, not to say downright worry in the hearts of those who love the faith is nothing new. I already have mentioned that I take the very word from the vocabulary of Saint Paul over 1,900 years ago. I might suggest that within the lifetimes of most living men the Church has been faced with crises, scandals, betrayals, compromises which which differ in no way, except perhaps by degree, from those which account for this solicitude. Some of these occasions for solicitude have been regional, but the region covered two-thirds of the world, as for example where established atheism has threatened to snuff out the light of faith in the years since 1920. Some have been local, as for example in the dreadful threat to the Church and its life in France during the first decade of this century, in Italy a generation before, in Germany at about the same time when Kulturkampf so gravely threatened the survival of Catholicism. Some of the threats have been worldwide and remarkably like certain of the worst aspects of the present crises, since the threat came not so much from without (attacks from without sometimes strengthen the faith) but from within, as it does now, and on the level of ideas and values profoundly challenged and, by attempt at least, discredited. Such was the Modernism which swept through the Catholic world like a contagion in the days of St. Pius X.

Obviously the mood of a somewhat morbid solicitude which grips hearts at the moment is best dispelled by faith, by greater faith if you already believe strongly, by better faith if you still retain any elements of that divine gift. "I believe, Oh Lord, help Thou my unbelief!" is a prayer which from the time it was written in the Sacred Scriptures has served to strengthen faith where it was under attack, and dispelled anxiety concerning the faith where it seemed warranted by disturbing events.

However not only faith but also the reading of a bit of history helps to put back into perspective the view of things which is so upset by the confusions of the moment and unsettled by the solicitude of those who must keep the faith through these hours of anxiety. I have special reasons, which speedily will become obvious, for choosing but one of several moments in history which have paralleled our own, both in their discouragement lest the faith be dying and in their tendency to fear that the end of all that we cherish must be close at hand. In the last 2,000 years there have been a score of such periods. I recall but one and I recall it because it so remarkably resembles in its mood and its elements our own moment of history.

Samuel Eliot Morison, one of the best read professors of history at Harvard, is the source of the recollection that the year 1492 was one of the most discouraged years in the history of Europe.

At the end of the year 1492 most men in Western Europe felt exceedingly gloomy about the future. They had ample reason to feel so. The princes and monarchs were in amazing degree mental cases and in any case were divided deeply from one another on the temporal and political level. Alexander VI was pope that year and all of us who were taught our history by certain Protestants or a special kind of Catholics, who are not "afraid to face the truth," know what a disaster that was — although, truth to tell, despite the morals of his early days and the manners of his family, I always have had a secret suspicion that he did a better job than he is generally attributed — but here I confess to prejudices which will come out later. In any case, in 1492 long-established institutions, ecclesiastical, academic and political, were decaying. Frustration was in the air. Well-meaning people were growing cynical or desperate. The limited in intellect were giving themselves up to vice and aimlessness. The sensitive and intelligent, appalled by the threats of the future and the problems of the present, tried to escape the solicitudes of 1492 by studying the classical pagan past.

This particular "flight from reality" turned out to be the source of a blessing in disguise for that is how the great Western Renaissance began. From the study of the pagan past they acquired

3

a new enthusiasm for beauty on the level of art, architecture and poetry. They began to create new music, new styles of life and above all they began to look for new frontiers, new worlds to conquer. Permit me to dwell on this for a moment because it provides a parallel well worth our meditation. The Nuremberg Chronicle, in a folio dated July 12, 1492, forecast that the end of the world in fire and flood could not possibly be far off.

I never look out the window of my office in Rome without thinking of that particular period of solicitude. It is an extraordinary antidote to any morbid solicitude which might overcome me as a result of the mail and the newspapers on my desk reporting the solicitudes of the present. The first thing I see as I look out my window is the dome of St. Peter's, one of the great monuments to the Renaissance that was the result, in the way I have indicated, of the discouragement of intelligent people over the seeming fate of the institutions—religious, cultural and other—which they cherished but considered to be doomed, so doomed that they turned from them to the study of classic antiquity.

Nearer to my window, a mere matter of a few feet from the window ledge, is one of the ends of Bernini's colonnade, another monument to the new beauty that grew out of the refuge from the old despair. It bears an inscription proclaiming its completion under Pope Alexander VII, who, a few years before, had served as papal nuncio in Westphalia, Germany, trying to bring to an end in the pattern of papal nuncios then and now the conflicts between the nations which added up to the Thirty Years War. His very name is a reminder to me that even wars come to an end so long as there are men working for peace somewhere loose in the world, and the things of art and science, such as account for Bernini's colonnade, are brought back into the service of a religion that was thought to be dying only a few years before.

The symptoms of that oncoming death in 1492 were again remarkably like the symptoms which many interpret as marking the end of institutional and revealed religion in our own day. It was a year of weird religious developments. All over Europe there were breaking out forms of witchcraft, black magic, aberrations of the religious instinct, underground movements and like religious abnormalities which, then as now, increased the solicitude in the hearts of believers. While the intelligent and sophisticated—always a minority—now as then—were taking refuge in the study of the ancient classics, the more simple-minded citizens of more primitive taste or instinct went in for astrology, contestation and general dissent.

I need not labor the parallel, need I, between 1492 and the present? The universal mood of dissent on the one hand and of anxiety on the other reveals its presence everywhere. You now see the first in the Piazza Navona and on the Spanish Stairs in Rome; you see the second at the Vatican. You see the first on the edges of Boston Common, on the corners of selected streets in San Francisco, or in any of the other places where either the "hippies" or the rebellious gather. You see the evidence of the solicitude on the faces of university presidents, wondering whether to send for the police, and you hear echoes of it in the speeches of the more intelligent of our political leaders. The rumor went around recently that the whole state of California was going to slide into the Pacific on April 15 that year—do you remember? As a devout New Englander I was deeply disillusioned by the newspapers dated April 16!

I need not speak of the resurgence of witchcraft. The newspapers have carried accounts of this nonsense in terms of a priest in England, an ex-priest and his wife in Switzerland, a series of soothsayers in Holland, orgies of a liturgical and even more debased kind hither, thither and yon, none of them new to the 1960s and 1970s but somehow characteristic of our times. There has been a dramatic resurgence of interest in astrology. Even newspapers which no longer carry essential information, like ship arrivals, and of course suppress any references to births or other heart-breaking news, carry columns providing astrological guides for each day.

If the political conflicts, religious confusion and intellectual decay did not lead you to the temptation to despair, the conversations with our teen-age children would, and so rather than abandoning yourselves to the dark arts, to witchcraft, to drugs or to hippiedom, you are looking for new interests, not so much in classical antiquity as in the new technology and the promise of the age of space. And although filled with solicitude, you are sustained by faith, by faith and a bit of history.

For suddenly in 1492 explorers began to open up not merely a new world but an entirely new perspective. In a couple of generations after the extraordinary exploit of Christopher Columbus, the mood of the whole world had changed. Missionaries were setting out for the ends of the earth and the foundations were being laid for a new type of civilization, of commerce, of exploration and discovery, which would not merely revolutionize but energize religion, politics and culture generally. The English produced fewer witches and gave us a run of poets, headed by Shakespeare. The French grew weary of their dissolute sorcery and gave us new art, new music, new poetry, new theater, new interests for all the world. The Spaniards and the Portuguese were hard at work, in a matter of years, building a future in the New World which would surpass even the best periods of their history in the Old World, at least in certain basic ways of service to all mankind, and there were born unbounding ambitions and inspired enthusiasms, producing a new period of exploration, discovery and civilization, as a result of a change of mood from defeatism and discouragement to hope and the desire for accomplishment. All this may be said, without undue simplification, to have been the result of the exploit of Christopher Columbus, sponsored by a believing queen.

At a given moment in 1492, in the midst of all the moaning and groaning, the Niña sailed slowly into the harbor of Lisbon with the news of the discovery of a New World. Historian Morison notes the "complete and astounding change that then took place." Sir Charles Oman declared: "A new envisagement of the world has begun and men are no longer sighing after the imaginary golden age that lies in the distant past but speculating as to the golden age that might possibly lie in the oncoming future."

It is a little too early to say whether, as a result of the recent exploits of the astronauts and the opening up of the new world of space, "a complete and astounding change" will take place and we suddenly will turn from the dissensions of the present and the hankering after the past to "the golden age that might possibly lie in the oncoming future." For my own part however, optimist that I am, I think that such will prove to be the case and that something like that which followed on the exploits of Columbus, perhaps something even greater, will follow on the journeys to the moon and the ventures into the depths of space beyond the moon. As a matter of fact I became certain of this while I was listening to the astronauts, symbols of the greatest potentials of our present-day scientific technology, reading from the first pages of Sacred Scripture, for all the world to hear, during their orbiting of the moon at Christmas time, on the Apollo flight.

One night in Rome I was present when Jim Lovell showed us the films of the landing on the moon, the first bus stop on the journey to the ends of creation. While he talked and we watched the first tentative steps on the dust of the moon's surface, I remembered a magnificent talk that Pope Pius XII gave a few months before he died, a talk in which he said that he could not understand the universal pessimism about the future, about the prospects for life and for all created things, in the hearts of people who are standing, as is our generation, on the shores of space, no longer with a little globe to conquer, occupy and exploit—but with the whole cosmos to make our own and, thanks to our new technology and, please God, reborn confidence in ourselves and in God, to bend to our purposes. Well I cannot understand such pessimism either—and it is not because I follow the pope (though I tend to

7

do so for excellent reasons) in his evaluation of the times, but because I have read the story of humanity's past, including 1492, and have sensed the direction of humanity's future, beginning with elements, wise and foolish, which are revealing themselves today.

Now let us bring these reflections a little more close to that which chiefly explains our solicitude, namely the Holy Catholic Church. Many share your anxiety over many things which are happening in the Church. You are deeply moved by a spirit of solicitude for your Holy Mother the Church. If you did not have such a mood, one might think that there was something the matter with your common sense, not to say your faith and your love. But if that mood were to overwhelm you, one would know for certain that there was something the matter with your hope as well as with your faith. One might also fear that you had lost your perspective and had so forgotten the history of your religious community, even in this area of the world, as to have become the victims of a "collective amnesia."

I suppose that everyone thinks that his diocese is having a rough time at the moment. I do not happen to know what is the nature of the particular problems of most American dioceses but I do know that, in the old phrase, there is no clause in Father Adam's will which exempts any of them from the troubles of this life, including the denial by some of our brethren of Father Adam himself!

Let us take a look at the history of one typical American diocese choosing that of Hartford because it is the home of your Knights of Columbus. The diocese of Hartford was established on Nov. 28, 1843 and the situation in the city of Rome, from which I have come in order to be with you, could not possibly have been less promising than it was in November 1843 when Pope Gregory XVI sat down to sign the document that brought this diocese into being. As a matter of fact one almost asks why he bothered to sign it; the future was so bleak. There was little chance, humanly speaking, that the venture would work out as it has done. There were revolutions all over the place and most of the people who were coming here were coming as voluntary or involuntary emigrants from lands where they were starving to death and subject to persecution largely because of their religion. As for Rome, on the very day of Pope Gregory's coronation, the ceremonies were interrupted by a group of what now would be called in Italy "manifestatori." The movement which they represented was determined at all costs to get rid of the pope, the papacy and all the "structures" leading to or from both. They were not fooling and, as a matter of fact, they were not entirely mistaken in some of the charges which added passion to their demonstrations, noisy protests and highly organized dissent.

In Hartford, as throughout New England, there are many descendants of those angry young men who gave Pope Gregory XVI and later Pope Pius IX a bad time. Some of those descendants are Knights of Malta. Most of them are Knights of Columbus. The overwhelming majority of them not only have long since settled for the institutional Church but are worried sick by the attitude toward it of those whom they regard as "new breeders" —not without reason for grave concern and sincere solicitude.

The other day there came to my office in Rome a very respectable Italo-American who, after a presentation of the woes and worries of the moment in his parish and diocese, ventured the suggestion that the bishop be removed, the auxiliary bishop transferred, the pastor fired and the parish committee dissolved. He also had a remark to make, to which I was by temperament more open, that the organist be deprived entirely of access to the choir loft. Despite the passion of his criticisms, there was no mistaking his love for the parish. I asked him how long he had lived in it and he replied that he had arrived in America from Italy only a very few years before and had taken up residence immediately in the parish to which he had become so devoted. I asked him from what town in Italy he came and when he told me I could not keep from thinking that it would have been absolutely impossible for his

9

great-grandfather not to have belonged to one or another of the anticlerical organizations of the 19th century, particularly the "carbonari." Here he was fighting to reform and preserve his parish out of sheer love for it, while his every ancestor in all probability would have devoted equal energy to destroying the parish where the family then lived and certainly to outlawing if not exiling the pope.

I mentioned this to him and he made an extremely interesting remark: "I have no interest in what my ancestors tried to do to tear down the parish church, but I will not permit the closing of the parish school in my parish at home or any change in the liturgy which makes my wife, my children and myself no longer feel at home in the parish church we love!"

Well, give him a thought or two when you are about to throw in the sponge because of seeming rejection of religion by your 18-year-old son immediately after his first introduction to what the professor is pleased to call the history of Europe or, even more sad, his theology professor has offered him as the secret of the universe!

The archdiocese of Hartford used to be part of the archdiocese of Boston in days which I found, generally speaking, abundantly satisfactory. Sometimes I hear rumors that the archdiocese of Boston is having troubles of one kind or another and, because I love it dearly for a thousand reasons this causes me great solicitude. But then, fortified by faith, I pick up the history book and there I read the archdiocese of Boston was established by Pope Pius VII. I'm afraid he had to delay the establishment of that ecclesiastical jurisdiction because he was having hell's own time with a man named Napoleon. As a matter of fact Napoleon had arrested him and held him captive, now in one place, now in another, usually in the snowy, inaccessible towns along the passes in the maritime Alps between Italy and France. In any case, on July 6, 1809 Pius VII was on his way into exile again under the political pressures of the times. One of the last things he did before he left was to authorize the establishment of the diocese of Boston, for which a large number of those present here in the hall, including myself, are deeply grateful to him. But the first bishop of Boston, Bishop Cheverus, who was a victim of the same revolutions in which Pius VII had been caught up, could not be consecrated for two years after his nomination because the exile of the pope made it impossible for them to get the proper documents.

Communications being what they then were, I do not know how worried the Catholics of Boston were during that period. Communications being what they are now, the sense of frustration, anxiety and sheer fury would have led to some strong feelings, unless the sentiment in Boston has changed considerably since I was transferred out of there a few years ago!

Do not misunderstand me. I am not denying the reality of the present troubles in the Church, nor am I minimizing them by a single degree. Most assuredly I am not mocking your worries or underestimating the grounds for your solicitude. I simply am pleading for the strengthening of your faith, the heightening of your hope, the maturing of your charity. Moreover I am suggesting that these desirable ends will be served by the remembrance of history, beginning with the histories of your own families. I hardly need tell you why the fathers and mothers, the grandfathers and grandmothers, the great-grandfathers and great-grandmothers of most of your families came here in the first place. They did not come here because they had no worries or solicitude at home and thought they would like a change in the places of their rejoicing, their affluence and their absence of cares. Neither did they come here gladly—or, more exactly, they did not leave their own countries gladly, not a bit of it. They came here in tears and in flight from Trouble, with a capital T, as the Irish always have given the word "trouble," and with a small "t" in the case of most other more ebullient nationalities. But it was trouble, no matter how you spelled it, in every case. Many of them thought the end of the world had come and their journey to America was made with heavy hearts. They went to work in the new world without much support from those who already were here and with very little with which to do the magnificent job that they did.

Let me now move to a discussion of what is my present work and why I ask you to pray for it, not because it is all that difficult, but because it is extremely important to you and to the renewal of the Church that is the object of your well-founded solicitude.

Contrary to a general impression, the congregation (or "ministry") of which I am president is not concerned exclusively nor even primarily with the problems of priests. Our congregation is concerned rather with what would be the solution of most of the problems of all of the priests who have problems if that solution were promptly worked out and promptly accepted. As a matter of fact our congregation is concerned with what would be the solution of most of the problems of most of the people I know, priests or laymen. It is concerned with work—in this case, the pastoral work of the clergy and, more particularly, that work of catechetics, the teaching of the faith, which is increasingly not only a concern but a responsibility of the laity.

Our congregation has for its competence the pastoral work of the Church, the everyday task of instruction in the faith (as distinct from debates concerning theology, which are the responsibility of two other congregations), the high privilege and tough job of making Jesus Christ better known and loved. If that work were being done as it should be done and can be done by all the priests in the world, we would have fewer problems. If we were all working at that full-time,—with our whole mind, our whole heart and all our soul—we would have no problems of the kind usually publicized. We would have problems of health perhaps, occasionally economics, budgeting of time and personality conflict because of the desire of each of us to do the job better than anyone else.

Accordingly, while there is a section in our congregation devoted to the life and ministry of priests as there is a section devoted to airport chapels and to pilgrimages for the increase of piety among the devout, the principal section, I would venture to say, is that given to the work of teaching and preaching the unfootnoted faith of our fathers. When I once spoke of this "unfootnoted faith" which is the primary object of our concern, I was taken to task by an American magazine which implied that this meant I was a hidebound conservative whose mind was utterly closed to the new theology and any of the new directions of things. The criticism was profoundly unfair—as I think the author knew—because nothing could be further from the truth. My point was that, whatever my personal recollections or prejudices, it is the Congregation for the Doctrine of the Faith that is responsible for the footnoted theologies, as is also the Congregation for Seminaries in no small degree. But our congregation is concerned with the preaching of the Catholic faith, the methods of teaching that faith, as it was transmitted from the Fathers.

If this work—the right word for which is evangelism—were being done day in and day out, every year, all over the world, priests would go to bed each night extremely tired, but they would wake to face a new day extremely exhilarated. This of course is true of all those, priests and laity, who take the Christian life seriously and seek to spread the faith. Busy priests may be tired priests; they may even occasionally be bewildered priests, bewildered by the sheer magnitude and the eternal implications of their work. But they are never problem priests.

In every corner of America, Canada and Mexico there are scores of these priests and you know them well. They are too busy with the problems of others, for such is their life and ministry, to be bothered about the problems of themselves. They suffer from no identity crisis. They know exactly why they asked for ordination and received it so gladly and so unselfishly. They are too preoccupied with bringing men to God and God to men to become the victims of purely personal, individual fits of self-pity or any other form of preoccupation with self. They are total men, totally given to the total service of the total community and the total Christ.

That means, to me at least, that they are saints and there are far more of them alive and at work in our dioceses and our parishes, despite all our problems, than we are inclined to think.

The part of the Knights of Columbus in building the climate which produces such priests has been enormous.

When I was a boy the Knights of Columbus in my home parish gave me, by word and example, encouragement which has shaped my life: encouragement in the practice of the faith, encouragement in solicitude for the interests of the Church which teaches the faith, example in the attitudes which should flow from the possession of the faith. For this I am thankful!

Throughout the years of my priesthood I have been inspired by the works of the Knights of Columbus, works of piety, works of instruction, works of mercy. I merely note such programs as the instructions in the faith provided by the Knights of Columbus by mail to all those who apply for such instruction; the inevitable presence of the Knights of Columbus to recite prayers for the dead at wakes; the special honors paid by the Knights of Columbus to the bishop of the diocese when he is present for a ceremonial occasion; the vigils in honor of the Real Presence of Christ in the Blessed Sacrament maintained on certain feast days by the Knights of Columbus as a group and individually. I mention merely in passing the fact that the local council of the Knights in my own home parish was the first council known to me to have among its officers the only black man who happened to be a member of our parish back in the 1920s and 1930s when, it is commonly asserted, we were living in a period of singular lack of sensitivity and fraternal instincts in our intergroup relations! For all these things I am thankful!

The ring on my finger is a gift from some Knights of Columbus in the council [No. 121, Brighton, Mass.] of which, as a priest of my native city, I am a member. That ring has of course intense overtones of personal sentiment, but as my episcopal ring it is also a symbol to me of an essential attribute of the Knights of Columbus: the desire to be identified with the hierarchy in all that the hierarchy is or exists to do for everyone within the Church and the general community.

As the bishop who founded the diocese of Worcester I have a special debt to the Knights of Columbus. The order there took the lead in helping me to build the new diocese committed to my care. They particularly identified themselves with the service of the cathedral as the center of the life of the diocese, with the works of our hospital and especially with the program for unwed mothers which we started in a remodeled and much beloved old New England house within the city limits of Worcester. I well remember how one Halloween night there had been rumors of disorders scheduled by the unruly for the area around that house. The young girls had heard the rumors and naturally were terrified. I did not call the police or any other special guards. I called the Knights of Columbus and they stood in the pouring rain all around the property on which the house stood until there no longer was danger of trouble.

In Pittsburgh among the first to call on me when I was transferred to that diocese were the leaders of the Knights of Columbus. The purpose of their visit was not merely to welcome me as the bishop but above all it was summed up in the only question that they put to me: "What special burden of yours do you wish us to help share? Where and how can we help?"

I had not been in Pittsburgh long enough to know all the needs of the diocese and so my answer was largely instinctive as indeed was their response. I said that I hoped to strengthen the existing program for retarded children, for children born with grievous handicaps and, as a result, "exceptional" in their educational needs and the development of their faculties and their personalities. I confessed that it would be difficult for me, a Catholic bishop, to get from the average foundation the kind of money to do the extra building, extra research, extra work of every kind to open up new frontiers of service to such children, service per-

15

formed of course chiefly and best by the Catholic sisters who have pioneered in this field of special education.

The meeting with the Knights did not last 30 minutes, but it would have taken 30 years for me to raise the kind of money that their subsequent hard work made available during the last 10 years—while they were at the same time taking care of their existing local commitments, national commitments, international commitments and other internal commitments, mostly religious, of the order.

As episcopal chairman of the Department of Social Justice in the United States Catholic Conference, it became my responsibility to launch a task force to help meet, in the name of the bishops, the problem of the inner city, with its overtones of group relations, color, poverty, juvenile delinquency and social decay which are now so familiar and so embarrassing to us all. It did not cross my mind to turn to a government agency, a philanthropic foundation or indeed the Bishops' Conference alone for the needed money? I put myself immediately in touch with your supreme knight, John McDevitt, and I asked him for a major part of the dough. He pointed out that he could not act independently, especially where money is concerned, but in no time the word came back that the Knights of Columbus had made a three-year pledge which in fact made the task force a possibility.

I had and have no illusion that this money was forthcoming because John McDevitt and I happen to be lifelong friends. It was forthcoming because that is the way the Knights of Columbus respond when the American bishops seek out their help.

The Knights of Columbus already had made possible for the service of the bishops and the Church the growing organization that is CARA—a coordinated effort to study scientifically exactly what are our technical problems, to get them down in black on white so that we can proceed in an orderly fashion to their intelligent as well as prayerful solution.

I have some idea of what the Knights of Columbus have

accomplished in the way of social work in Canada, in Mexico and therefore throughout all of North America. I came here to say "thank you" for all this.

When I was a young priest who knew no one and whom no one knew I was eager to help promote a climate for peace as soon as possible after World War II. The first meeting for such a project I ever attended was under the auspices of the Knights of Columbus. It was in New York City and had been convoked by Judge John Swift. Dr. George Herman Derry was chairman of the Knights of Columbus peace program and that program, immediately following World War II, was my introduction to a series of peace projects, Catholic, civic and ecumenical with which I have been identified ever since. I owe the Knights of Columbus a word of thanks for their part in that chapter of my life.

As an American bishop I am grateful for the bell tower that the Knights of Columbus erected in our national capital and on the grounds of our Shrine to the Immaculate Conception, patroness of our nation. That tower is not a symbol of any kind of triumphalism (as is sometimes alleged) and it is in no sense a waste of money. It is a symbol of all the values of which bell towers in every corner of the world and from the earliest beginnings have been the effective symbols: the need that men and nations be called constantly to the worship of God, the need for reminders of God's presence among us and of God's Providence over us, most especially in those places otherwise given up to the sounds of voices which speak for purely personal, partisan, temporal or otherwise less than fully human hopes.

Coming from Rome, I must thank you for what the Knights of Columbus have done there: for what they did in making possible the so modern shortwave transmitter for the Vatican Radio, so necessary to bring the message of the Holy See beyond the various curtains which have fallen between some nations and their brethren elsewhere; for what they provided in the way of playgrounds and programs for underprivileged children in the crowded, problem-ridden center of Catholic Christendom. Coming from Rome, I owe you thanks no less fervent for all that you have done in the name of the Catholic Church in other parts of the world where war always has occasioned the solace to the afflicted which has characterized the Knights of Columbus wartime and postwar programs, the latest example of which is their generosity through the Holy Father to the people of Biafra.

May I say a particular word of thanks for the editorial policies of your publication, COLUMBIA, and particularly for your recent support of the Church in her position in defense of human rights, human dignity and human life itself? One must applaud particularly your defense of life in its very beginnings, where God may wish it, against the objective evil that is contraception, as well as your defense of life in its growth to birth against the brutal evil that is abortion.

Is there anyone here present who regrets having been born? The very ultimate in melancholic-depressed insanity would be the expression of the wish that you had never been born. Everybody loves life, at least his own. Such a love is instinctive. The Knights of Columbus have tried to communicate that love for the individual person who happens to have had the good luck to be born to all those whose gift of life is threatened by the planned economies, purely political aid programs and coldly materialistic programs respecting conception and birth which are abroad at the moment.

Speaking of the defense of life, to the conception and birth of which you have been loyal in such strongly Christian terms, there is one other aspect of its primacy about which I would like to speak very briefly and without any offense. I might wish that the Knights of Columbus, in their local councils and in their solemn assemblies throughout the country, were as alert and articulate about some of the other threats to life, particularly the lives of adults when nations have recourse to war, as they are, and very properly are, in the case of the lives of children. The Knights of Columbus always have been wise to the threats to life in its begin-

nings—to the contraceptive campaign, to the abortion campaign
and all the little schemes related to both, but I wish you were
equally alert and equally articulate to the prodigal manner in which
life suddenly becomes dispensable once war becomes an instrument of national policies or the means to settling international
disputes.

Recently I have found it extremely interesting to notice how
many of the same names appear on, let us say, the boards of direc-
tors of the World Population Control Board, the commissions for
aid to Latin America and other impoverished zones and, with
marvelous consistency, in those posts or rooms of the Pentagon
where it is decided how many hundreds of thousands of young
men's lives are "dispensable" in order to gain a given hilltop in
Southeast Asia—to cite an imaginary example—or to make the
world safe for democracy in other parts of the world. Is it not
strange that those—I name no names—who as men in control of,
let us say the World Bank or the Defense Department or the World
Population program, so frequently turn out to be the same men—
not to say the same man? Is it not curious how grateful they are—
or he is—in various parts of the world and under various political
systems, to the parents who had the boys who grew up to be
soldiers, while at the same time hoping that the soldiers, in the
happy chance that they survive, go home to sterilized wives and
to nuptial love productive of no new life?

This is one of the mysteries that I submit for your meditation
when you are formulating resolutions about war and peace, about
taking a "positive attitude" toward governmental programs for
birth control in Latin America, among Negroes, in poor districts,
and in the parts of the world which depend upon us for considerably more than powdered milk, abortion pills, contraceptive de-
vices and study clubs in how to be sterile, though married, and
happy, though the victims of an unholy system that is antilife,
antihuman and, since we are talking within the privacy of a Catholic den and therefore may indulge our little prejudices, anti-God.

19

The antilife mood of our civilization includes many militaristic aspects to which we Knights of Columbus have not been as sensitive as we have been to the antibaby movements. Accordingly I ask you, the representatives of the largest and best organized group supporting the United States bishops, to master and to implement in its totality their pastoral letter of November 1968 on Human Life in Our Day. You already have defended the part of it that supports the Holy Father in his encyclical on Human Life. Study carefully and help make effective the second part of it which follows the lead of the Holy Father in his plea for peace and for protest against the horror that is war. Contempt for human life has become, in our technocratic civilization, an across-the-board thing. So the defense of human life never must be selective, as it is in the case of many people, not merely liberals but also conservatives. We must be against the slaughter of innocent life in every form or our case is insincere and illogical concerning the specific threat to life that we choose to be touchy about. You must be against whatever is antilife in modern military, medical, surgical, political or family morality. You must be for whatever promotes life—all across-the-board. Selective liberals, selective conservatives, selective partriots and selective lovers leave something to be desired.

You must say Yes to technology designed to find effective ways of exploiting space, of using science, of probing the ocean, of making the desert flower in order to provide whatever food may be needed for that banquet of life to which all are invited. You must say No to whatever technology prevents life, destroys life or maims life—whether in the act of love, or in the womb of a mother, or in the building of peace and the correcting of international injustices. You must say Yes to any diplomatic means, judicial means, medical means or other means by which life is fortified. You must say No to things like napalm, concentration camps, slums, denial of opportunity to love within marriage, if one chooses marriage, and to cooperate with the creative power of God in producing life as well as the providential power of God in preserving it.

Together with your bishops and the pope, you must take a consistent, across-the-board, positive position in favor of life—life in its beginning, life in its growth, life in its education, life in its prospering, life in its freedom and immunity from external compulsions or dangers to its integrity, life as long as you can keep life alive—and you cannot compromise it at any point or you undermine your position from the very beginning and all across-the-board.

Because you say Yes to life and No to its prevention or destruction, you must support new ways to produce food, as through the wonders of the developing oceanography, the untold treasures of what are now the jungles of India, Africa and Latin America, all to the end that those jungles may become orchards, the lunar landscapes of places like Peru may become gardens, the deserts may become attractive, the battlefields may become extinct and life may become once again no longer a thing of tension and anxiety, but a thing of joy, beginning with birth—formerly called, by the way, a "happy event" in decent families.

Above all we never must allow slogans like "too many mouths to feed" to justify our prevention of life, or slogans like "my country, right or wrong" to justify our wars against life. We never must allow love for self or love for country to silence our deeper loyalties to life and to God's law. The world could become, you know, a graveyard by so-called "democratic processes" just as quickly as it could by nazi processes—especially if science in its various forms and personal morality is allowed to become autonomous— no longer responsive to the common good, to the Providence of God or to God Himself—let alone our neighbor.

As men unqualifiedly on the side of life you must oppose loyally and positively but implacably any policies or any programs which would decide who is to be born or from whom new life is to come. We must defend our brothers, once they are born, when the suggestion comes that they may be "expendable" for policy reasons unexplained and unacceptable. As we defend our brothers

21

unborn, and while we may react positively to those elements of government programs which are on the side of life, we must react negatively and boldly to any parts of government programs or private programs, programs at home or abroad, which threaten life, threaten to crush it out with abortion or threaten its future by controlling the freedom of people to perpetuate their kind, threaten this freedom by pressures or techniques contrary to God's law. And we must not get fooled by any talk about God's Providence in these matters! Not long ago the contraceptionists among Catholics used to say that we traditionally left too much to the "Providence of God" and that they were weary of this phrase. Parenthood, they said, should be "responsible"—which means the free result of human and autonomous choice.

Anyone in his right mind will agree—so long as love for life is not smothered in the life of love. But be on guard against a new appeal that is being made forsooth to the "Providence of God," such an appeal as showed up amazingly in a speech at Notre Dame University when a powerful politician said in effect: "Now it is in the Providence of God that we should work with those who are trying to ration life, where once it was in the Providence of God that we increase and multiply!" Policies have changed, at least on the lips of politicians, clerical and lay. The Providence of God has not, except, again, in the minds of time-servers, clerical or lay.

You have asked that I include a quick view of the personality and work of the contemporary papacy and pope.

Jacques Maritain, probably the most intelligent layman of our century, once said of these modern popes that there is no greater evidence of the presence of the Holy Spirit among us than the luminous teachings, examples and characters of the popes in his own lifetime: Leo XIII, St. Pius X, Benedict XV, Pius XI, Pius XII, John XXIII and Paul VI—no two alike in temperament, in background or in charismatic gifts, but no one repudiating the teachings or policies of another, nor disagreeing with another, or breaking faith with the others. And so, I would find it difficult to express differences with the pope or to speak unfavorably of his leadership and his teaching. Attribute my deep-seated prejudice for the pope not to lack of intellectual independence or the "American" spirit, but to the kind of confidence which prompted Maritain's remark. Maritain's judgment, I am confident, will also be that of history, once the tumult and the shouting have died, about the alleged "political" inadequacies of Pope Pius XII, let us say; the excessive simplicities, as is sometimes pretended, of Pope John XXIII, or the failure to be "with it" of Pope Paul when "mods" are pressing for novel and "more contemporary" approaches to ancient threats to liberty, to love and to life itself, not to mention to the faith.

I would take my place by Catholic instinct at Cardinal Newman's side when he argued that the burden of proof—and that proof must be clear, considered and weighed long and prayerfully—is always on the side of those who presume to take their stand against the pope, even on a point of policy, let alone faith and morals even as proclaimed by his ordinary teaching authority, even without infallibility. And so by instinct but also for solid theological reasons I take my stand on the side of the pope in any of the present crises, questions or controversies—whether with respect to morality, to sound doctrine or to social order. No mere counting of heads, even usually bright heads, would embarrass me in my instinctive response to so much of the dictates of faith and so many of the lessons of history. Nor is this because I am a member of the Roman curia, a bishop or a Knight of Columbus. This instinct, not only associated with a fascination which the papacy merely as an historical phenomenon always has had for me, dates back over most of the years of my life as, I suspect, it does over most of the years of the lives of most Catholics.

In my own case it found expression at every stage of my life as a Catholic: In high school days I was a one-man vigilance committee in the public school I attended to make sure that, whatever else they said about the Church, they never attacked the pope without my asking, "When did he say that? On what page of what book do you find it? What were the circumstances of the times?"

In the years of college I remember the voice of Pope Pius XI coming over the radio for the first time in history that the chief shepherd of all the world was heard by all the world as he spoke. Back in those early days of radio, some of us listened at stores and garages to hear the voice of the pope. Nothing I have heard since on radio has thrilled me as much.

In seminary days, at audience in St. Peter's or at the Vatican, I heard Pius XI speak against totalitarianism and the threat of war and Pius XII speak of the dignity of the person and the essential elements of eventual world peace.

In graduate days, as a priest-student, I did special studies on the resistance of the papacy to modern nationalism, militarism, impersonalism and the other forces destructive of religious piety, the primacy of the person and the spiritual elements of the common good.

In youthful days of priesthood I wrote on the pope and the war, the necessity for the Vatican as an oasis of sanity in a world chaotic with nationalistic rivalries and conflicting imperialisms.

As a young Bishop I used to love to preach on the Roman spirit and the manner in which it rebuked and refined a certain parochialism, chauvinism, ghetto and parochial mentality which so often characterized our own and other Christian peoples.

All this, again as by instinct, I linked not so much to any pope as a person, nor to the Roman Church as an institution, passionately though I loved and love it, but to Christ of whom the bishop of Rome is the vicar. Hence, I sometimes think, the instinct which made me choose my motto as a bishop: "Resonare Christum (corde Romano)"—"To echo Christ (with a Roman heart.)"

I beg the Knights of Columbus and all believers to bring an American mind and American heart to the problems of the Church and the world, but I beg you not less to bring a Roman heart to the problems of the Church in America. The Church, in a sense that may be discussed and of course must always be defined, can only be Roman and Catholic; you must keep it Catholic by the intensification of the strength, the prestige and the faith and works of your own diocese and of every other diocese. You must keep it Roman by your loyalty, as individuals, as diocesans and as an order, to the Holy Father.

The local Church is not the total Church, though the whole Church is at work in the local Church and vice versa. And the Catholic Church is not the antithesis of the Roman center of the Roman Church. The universal and the one, the worldwide and the local, are reconciled and blended in the Holy Roman Catholic Church.

And so I accept with joy the invitation to speak a brief word or two about the work of Pope Paul, what he is doing in our day in behalf of the universal Church from his base at the center of its unity.

What he is doing can be summed up under a few headings:

I. Certain gestures:

1. Pope Paul is a man who apparently finds it more easy to express by "gestures" the hopes that he and millions share for the Church in the world, hopes which elude all mere words and bypass long speeches. For instance, the rings he gave to all the bishops at the end of the Second Vatican Council and the matching ring that he himself wears all the time, an inexpensive and very simple ring, a symbol of that fraternity in the faith and the work which we really mean by collegiality. He asked all of us to wear it, certainly on certain occasions, as a symbol of fraternity as well as fealty.

2. The ring he gave the archbishop of Canterbury, on the spur of the moment, as the archbishop of Canterbury was getting into a car to leave St. Paul's in Rome. Pope Paul took off his ring spontaneously and handed it to the Anglican prelate as a symbol of ecumenism and of the prayer that we all may be one.

25

II. The journeys he has made, with such fatigue but with such obvious purposefulness, to the roots of our Christian heritage in Jerusalem the first year he was elected so that he might meet there the ecumenical patriarch of the Orthodox Church; to the UN so that he might demonstrate our desire not to come to terms with the spirit of the world but to play our part in the building of a better world; the trip to Bombay to show that our sympathies go way beyond the usual geographical limits of traditional Christendom; to Fatima to remind us that prayer helps too and that there are certain centers where we pray with greater piety; to Istanbul in order that he might build up the prestige of his Orthodox brother, the ecumenical patriarch, who lives under conditions so perilous to Christianity; to Latin America to dramatize the problem of poverty and refresh the faith in a tired continent; to Geneva, the historic center of Protestantism, to bear his honest, brave witness both to his own position in conscience and to his affectionate respect for theirs, but above all to demonstrate that ecumenism at the moment is best realized in collaboration with one another, Catholic and Protestant, in the support and promotion of sound social movements; to Africa both to help create a climate of peace in that troubled continent and to pray at the shrines of the saints whose blood will be the seed of the Church in that continent which many believe, I am one, will be without doubt the continent of the 21st century.

The reactions throughout the world have been one of the greatest grounds for our hope for the future of the organized Church—and there is by the way no other known to historic Christianity than the organized Christian community. It is hard to understand why some Catholics fail to see this, while other Christians and even non-Christian believers in God so often perceive this so clearly. And so when Pope Paul walked in before the leaders of the Protestant world and said to them, "My name is Peter," Eugene Carson Blake, far from taking offense, saw that line as being in the same spirit as that of Pope John when he told a group of Jews who came to see him: "I am Joseph, your brother."

III. His teachings: Pope Paul has set forth honestly and exactly the terms on which and on which alone he could talk conscientiously while at the same time teaching with faith, charity and hope. His teachings, encyclicals and conferences, all without exception, are geared to this idea we have been talking about: life and life more abundant—life itself in the encyclical *Humanae Vitae;* life abundant in the encyclical on *The Progress of Peoples.*

Then almost every Wednesday he talks to the pilgrims who come to Rome about some aspect of the personality and the teachings of Jesus Christ, the life of every Christian person and institution.

IV. His clear desire is to implement Vatican Council II. His reform, if you like, of the curia (I would be more inclined, using the more usual vocabulary of a Catholic, to say his "renewal" of its original purposes). The patience with which he tries to ride the storms of the hour. The silence in the face of attack and of misunderstanding, a silence reminiscent of the lines of Scripture which recall how, in the face of calumny, "Jesus kept silent."

V. Finally his determination to do these things with courage, without compromising faith and without yielding to pressures, political or religious, other than those of conscience and the will of God, with which conscience must correspond at all times. This of course has been implicit in his encyclicals and in his pronouncements.

Well, what am I getting at? I am trying to beg you in this time of turbulence, this time of great solicitude as we said in beginning, but also this time of fantastic promise for the Church, for your bishops and, above all, for future golden ages to come, the magnificence of which we cannot even dream: to keep close to the pope as the living, visible, audible symbol of the whole thing! Don't take too seriously these distinctions between the periphery of the Church and the center of the Church. No one is at the periphery of the Church who is alive with its life of faith and love.

27

There is no periphery. If you are in it at all, you are at the center. The Church is not a pie with a center, a periphery and arguable portions—whether in the nonbeliever's sense of a "pie in the sky" or in the sense of some believers that it is a kind of pie measured as other things created or "cooked up." The Church is the single, living unified Body of Christ at work in the world; as a "body" it has parts but they are not dismembered. Christ is all and in all— not perfectly yet but more than the half-hearted think.

I used to love to hear read, during the ceremonies at the end of Masses on great feasts the papal blessing with its references to the local church: "this Holy Church of Worcester," "this Holy Church of Hartford," "this Holy Church of Philadelphia," "this Holy Church of San Francisco." Be proud of the local church to which you belong, but don't think of it as only a periphery.

If your local church is in communion with Rome, it is so intrinsically, so essentially, so vitally united to the center that it is all one, even as there is no divided Jesus Christ, the source and center of the Church of Hope.

II
Teachers of the Faith

To those of you to whom the commission to teach the faith has been entrusted—and that means every believer—I might address the encouragement of St. Paul to the Romans while offering these thoughts that they "might impart some spiritual grace to you, to strengthen you, that is, that among you I may be comforted together with you by that faith which is common to us, both yours and mine." (Romans 1, 11-12).

You have a lofty mission; you have a sublime task: to communicate the divine doctrine to men and teach them the certain road to everlasting happiness . . . in other words, to convey not just "theology" in the more technical sense of that word, not ever more refined "theologies," but the faith. Your mission is not to convey some professional theologian's point of view—however good it may be—or to indulge—as he may indulge—in speculations about the faith, but to communicate it as witnesses, as prophets, to convey the simple, clear and direct word of God himself, to give evidence of the Way, of the Life, of the Truth. The Lord Jesus was never a professional theologian. He was—he is—and always shall be a witness, a prophet of certain truths, which are largely inexplicable. Believe me, you are not so much theologians as witnesses, teachers of faith who are continuing his mission of testimony in the world of today.

It is quite true that even after his secession (apostasy) from God through Adam's sin, man kept and still keeps his capacity and the possibility to recognize the Lord through reason and turn to him as to his beginning and his end through natural will (cf. Romans, cap. 1, 2, 3). But it is likewise true that in the divine plan for redemption the ordinary and necessary means for saving mankind consists in evangelization, preaching, catechesis, that is, communication of the divine revelation.

Human philosophy could be the suitable and capable means for promoting research and knowledge of God (cf. 1 Corinthians 1, 21). It could be; but in fact, as St. Paul said, men *"evanuerunt in cogitationibus suis"*—men became foolish in their thoughts—(Romans 1, 21); they changed the very truth of God into lying" (ibid., 25).

It is not man's philosophy or science which reach true knowledge of God. Consequently, "it pleased God to save men through the foolishness of preaching" (1 Corinthians 1, 21). And it will not be man's efforts and works that will open the gates of everlasting happiness to him: "not by reason of good works which we did ourselves, but according to his mercy, he saved us through the waters of regeneration and renewal by the Holy Spirit; whom he has abundantly poured out in us through Jesus Christ our Saviour, in order that, justified by his grace, we may be heirs in the hope of life everlasting" (Titus 3, 5-7).

The necessity for evangelization and catechesis derives from these two facts: on the one hand man's practical impossibility of knowing the truth concerning his eternal destinies on the other hand, free and merciful divine giving, which has called and raised up man to cause him to participate in his inward life: *"divinae consortes naturae"* (II Peter 1-4) and his happiness: "we shall be like him, because we shall see him as he is" (I John 3, 2).

It is clear that it is not possible to know and believe the truths manifested by the Lord and admit and receive Christ's divine mysteries unless we have proper understanding of them, consequently unless we have the necessary corresponding evangelization.

The Apostle Paul plainly said so: "How then are they to call upon him in whom they have not believed? But how are they to believe him whom they have not heard? And how are they to hear, if no one preaches?" (Romans 10, 14).

God's sincere will that all men shall be saved was affirmed by the Apostle (cf. 1 Timothy 2, 4) and is clearly and securely founded in Jesus' command to preach the gospel to all people (cf. Matthew 28, 17). All, from the Apostles down to the last catechist in the most obscure village in the world, who devote themselves to this evangelization, are carrying out Jesus' command, cooperating in the salvation of all. You are amongst those, and I greet you as teachers of the faith. You are teachers of the faith because you tell people of something which they cannot acquire on their own; you are teachers of faith, because you set men upon the way to "the substance of things to be hoped for" (Hebrews 11, 1), and accompany them on the road toward the mastery of that truth by faith.

It is said that people, especially young people, are looking for concreteness and authenticity. This is true. But we must remember that man has always wished to try to touch and experiment with whatever he sees and whatever comes into his mind, whether such "concrete experience" be for better or for worse.

Adam recklessly put out his hand to the forbidden fruit; unbelieving Thomas put his finger in the divine Redeemer's wounds; man has always desired and always tried to find out for himself, not only in theory, but by making a practical test of concrete reality.

This perennial need has increased or has at least been accentuated, and man, especially young mankind, will not admit anything unless he can try and see for himself. Hence contestation, even insensate and violent contestation, protest against everything which is not clear, which cannot be proved by experience to be concrete, consistent, real and authentic.

Indeed ground is being gained by the tendency to derive the truths of being from the subject itself (subjectivism); and to derive norms for action and conduct from existence itself (existentialism). No more instruction and indoctrination from the exterior, no more imposition from outside, but development and assertion of the indi-

31

vidual, with more unforeseeable and anarchical results than ever.

That much applauded development of one's own capacities, one's own aspirations, one's own rights, which is so widespread at all levels and in all sectors, more or less derives from the supposition that man is himself the principle of his being and his doing. As you well know, the true, authentic reality is very different, because man is dependent in his being, just as he is dependent in his doing.

Others do not go so far as to derive and borrow everything from man as subject, but try, and make industrious efforts, to measure God by their own yardsticks and cut him down to their size. Their intention, or rather their excuse, is to adapt presentation and formulation of the truths to the modern mind; they end by forging a God to their own and others' liking. So we are faced with troubling silences and grave mutilations concerning fundamental truths of the faith and the Church's traditional testimony.

A God with no angels and no miracles, a man called Jesus, in whom the godhead was at work; a Virgin with no divine supernatural motherhood. All these and many other concepts destroy God; at least the "new" God is not the God of Abraham, of Isaac and of Jacob; of Peter, of Paul, of the Christian saints; of the faith of our fathers.

The tendency to wish to be like God is very ancient, and so is the wish to mould a God to our own taste. Pagan mythology proves it; Christian heresy confirms it. St. Hilary of Poitiers stood up against this temptation, and this tendency: *"quorum impietas est, Deum non ex ipsius professione, sed ex arbitrii sui voluntate metiri: ignorantes non minoris impietatis esse Deum fingere quam negare"* (In Ps. 1, 3; P.L. 9, 252). Their impiety consists in measuring God not by what he has said of himself, but by their own preferences, forgetting that describing God mendaciously is just as bad as denying him.

Those who put God aside in order to put man in his place— even though they may still speak of Jesus—those who forge a God to please themselves, are certainly not authentic teachers of the faith. A god who is the result of pseudo-mathematical speculations —the god of the philosophers—even though he be a cosmic god, or a poetic god, the "Alpha and Omega" of other created things— is not that God who shines in every page of Holy Scripture and who transcends not only me and my country, and my culture, but also all history and all creation, of which I am only the slightest part.

Authentic is equivalent to genuine. Water is genuine and pure when it gushes from a spring and without being altered or polluted arrives at our lips to quench our thirst and refresh us. Authentic and genuine doctrine is that which gushes from the spring and reaches our minds without being altered, without being mixed, without being polluted, and enlightens it; it reaches our heart and liberates it. St. Paul had to speak of the very many who already in his time were adulterating God's word; he contrasts his own sincere manner of speaking with theirs. He spoke from God, before God, in Jesus: *"Non sumus sicut plurimi, adulterantes verbum Dei, sed ex sinceritate, sed sicut ex Deo, coram Deo, in Christo loqui-mur"* (II Corinthians 2, 17). We are not as many others, adulter-ating the word of God; but with sincerity, as coming from God, we preach in Christ, in God's presence.

Fidelity to doctrine can and often ought to reach the point of fidelity to the formulation consecrated by the Church and by usage, even to the point of fidelity to single words. This not only because of what is contained in Scripture, of which not a jot or tittle shall pass away, (cf. Matthew 5, 18); but also because of the formula-tion of fundamental truths, which have been set forth and conse-crated by the magisterium and the Church's tradition.

To take an example, *consubstantial* is not simply of the same substance, and *transubstantiation* cannot be replaced by transfinali-zation or transignification. Of course, formulations, expressions and words are not the truths and the realities in themselves, yet they are authoritative statements of them and the means of reaching them, in such a way that our mind may safely grasp the truths and realities themselves, in so far as it is given to the limited human intellect to do so.

The much applauded theological explosion can sometimes be dangerous and have harmful effects, because new presentation, different formulation or replacement of a consecrated and defined term, can misrepresent the essential truth.

Besides this authenticity, which I would describe as objective, teachers of the faith must have an authenticity that I would call personal and interior. I was not educated in a Catholic elementary school, but I thank the Lord for having in my youth come under the formative influence of educators who were *persons* not *personages*—of deep Christian faith.

One episode in particular has remained stamped in my inmost soul and I still feel the impression of the moment when it occurred.

One of the boys in our class died, aged about eleven. Our religion teacher took us to visit and pray around his body. While we all were standing there in dismay and silence looking at our classmate and friend's immobile face, she, the teacher, said, with unforgettable power, warmth and love, but above all faith: "Stephen is not dead. It doesn't matter what things seem; he is alive. He is alive in God!"

She went on speaking with such inward, profound conviction, about Holy Scripture, the evidence given by the saints, and, with such persuasive force, of life in God—not the permanence of our little contribution to history, nor of our immortality in our descendants and in our achievements—poor Stephen had none of those things—but of our life in Jesus, thanks to baptism, our life in God, thanks to Jesus, who having died and risen again, will die no more. The way she spoke and what she said left an indelible impression on us. She was an authentic teacher of religion: she had, she lived, she sensed the faith; she conveyed Christian belief by means of a kind of healthy, creative and evangelical contagion of faith, which not even the most boring kind of "theology" has been able to kill, at least in me.

34

This is what I mean when I speak of authenticity, of inward genuineness. The Church's truths and realities are not only the object of abstract knowledge, but are lived, are tasted in the depths of the soul. St. Gregory the Great said: *"Quilibet predicator verba dare auribus potest, corda aperire non potest"* (Moral XXIX, 16). But if the preacher can only speak words to the ear and not open the heart, experience shows that the effect is very different according to who says the words. The effect is not bound to the words, but to the person who utters them. A master of pedagogy of other days said: "it is easier to instruct than to educate. In order to instruct it is enough to know something and know how to convey it; to educate you must be someone" (Adalbert Stifter). If this is true for natural, social and civil education, it is even truer of spiritual, supernatural training for the life of faith.

To be someone spiritually, interiorly, is not easy, and not a light, short-term matter. The Divine Master points to one way only, one means only of being someone in him and bringing forth much fruit for him: of being living roots. *"Ego sum vitis, vos palmites; qui manet in me, et ego in eo, hic fert fructum multum; quia sine me nihil potestis facere"* (John 15, 5). I am the wine, you are the branches; who remains in me and I in him, he brings forth much fruit; for without me you can do nothing.

In action it is of the greatest importance to know the nature and the end of one's acts. In our case we have to know the nature and the purpose of catechesis in teaching religion. You know more about these things than I do, because you have been studying them deeply for a long time and in the light of the new sciences. I will just make a few brief observations, in order to give you a fuller idea of what I think.

As you know, there are various differing ideas about the nature of catechesis. Some understand it—perhaps we may say, used to understand it—as teaching and training, most often solely by rote, in the first fundamental elements of the truths of the faith. Others consider it as an authoritative and official statement of salvation (such as is made by a herald), and that this has to receive assent, faith from man. Others again regard it as a cordial family conversation which ought to be engaging and convincing. Finally, some think of it as initiation and guidance to practice of Christian life.

There is some truth and something useful in all these concepts, so long as we bear the true and proper purpose of catechesis well in mind. It is not simply a matter of teaching something, of imparting new concepts, catechism formulas, passages from Holy Scripture and the liturgy. All these things are serviceable and necessary, but they are not the substance. The substance is to lead to the faith, to lead to life, to lead to love of God. The great Augustine put it this way. *"Hac ergo dilectione tibi tamquam fine proposito quo referas omnia quae dicis, quidquid narras ita narra ut ille cui loqueris audiendo credat, credendo speret, sperando amet"* (De catechizandis rudibus: cap. IV). Make love of God your aim and to it refer everything you say; everything you relate, relate in such a way that he who hears you may believe, believing may hope, and hoping may love.

True catechesis is therefore not simply a matter of reaching and believing some truths; it is an introduction and an encounter, a demonstration and a reception, a gift and an act of loving God. Augustine himself explained the distinction between believing in God and believing God: "this is God's work, that we may believe in him whom he had sent" (John 6, 29). He says, that you may believe in him, not that you may believe him. It is true that if you believe him you will also believe in him. But it is true that the devils believe him, but do not believe in him. With reference to the Apostles we can say in the same way. We believe Paul, but not in Paul: we believe Peter, but not in Peter.

Whoever believes in him who makes the impious man just, his faith is imputed to him for justice (Romans 4, 5). So what does believing in him mean? It means: by believing, loving; by believing, being devout; by believing, turning to him and incorporating ourselves among his members. This is the faith that God requires from us" (In. Jn. trat. XXIX, 6).

I said before that people, especially young people, desire and need concreteness and authenticity. Well, what is more concrete, more authentic than God? You have the great mission of giving God, in catechesis, in teaching religion, God as he is, as he has been revealed, as he has manifested himself, as his beloved Son made him known to us. This is why I spoke at some length about authenticity in teachers of the faith, because they have to communicate God just as he is, and have to communicate him frankly (with *parrhesia*) and forcefully (with *energia*), for these are characteristics of God's word. In other terms, you have to teach in such a way that those who are listening to you will not merely feel the bare and simple word of man in you, but the word of God. St. Paul thanked the Lord and praised the Thessalonians because they received his word as God's word: "for this we give thanks ceaselessly to the Lord because you received the word of God which you heard from us, you received it not as the word of men, but (which it truly is) as the word of God, which works in you, which you have believed" (1 Thessalonians 2, 13).

The question of the content of catechesis is a topical one. People used to argue about how to teach, now they are arguing about what to teach and are drawing up catechisms for different ages, sectors and milieux. I will not go into this matter now, for it needs to be examined thoroughly. Before I end, I will only indicate a number of fundamental themes, which all teachers of the faith should keep in mind. When I say all I mean all—from the Supreme Pontiff down to the last Bantu catechist, from the bishop to the priests in charge of the most remote of his parishes.

There is much talk of the Spirit nowadays but some of that talk is misleading rather than helpful. Indeed I have seen the question "Who is the Holy Spirit?" answered in a little Italian catechism with the words "He is my big mate"! I really don't know how a child can be led to worship the Holy Spirit when he is described to him in such terms. It escapes me how a child can take such a God seriously, presented to him like that.

Then there is more and more talk, and it is not without deep interest, of what is called Catholic Pentacostalism, and several like spiritualist movements—not to call them movements of the spirit.

But what I want to point out, and indeed, with force, is that the principal and fundamental subject of every catechesis is Jesus, his divine person, his preaching, his expiatory death, his resurrection, his ascension, his presence amongst us—in people who have need of us—in his People, acquired with his blood, in his organized and organic Church, in the "Paraclete" diffused *in cordibus nostris,* whom he promised and sent, in the Eucharist, as described so beautifully in the old Italian folk hymn, *Gesú Sacramentato.* In every case, always the center: Jesus!

Apostolic preaching, the early Church's catechesis converted the pagan world. What was it but presenting Jesus and reporting his life and works? Who or what will ever be able to give a renewed Christian spirit to this age of ours, if not Jesus, if not the presentation, the gift of Jesus? Not only the Jesus of the gospel according to St. Matthew, but also the Jesus of the experiences and meditations of St. John; of St. Paul, of mystics, of poets, saints and of us sinners, right down to today.

Before he begins anything else, in his Prologue St. John answers the question, "Who is Jesus?" He is the Word of God; the incarnate Word, the Word full of grace and truth.

It is fundamental and essential in every catechism to teach and cause people to feel who Jesus is: God—Man, and Redeemer of all, especially now that some have reached the point of rejecting (that is not too strong a word) the Incarnation and all theology based on this unutterable mystery. These are much worse than the old iconoclasts, for they are trying to destroy not so much the figure and the image as the person and the very reality of Jesus.

It is indispensable to present the Church's nature, her constitution, her work and her purpose. I do not mean the Church in her outward and (in the legitimate sense) historical form, but her spiritual, supernatural activity, her essence as the Mystical Body, of which Christ is the Head, which he left here upon the earth, organized in history, visible in human society.

Much of the doctrinal and practical confusion concerning the Church and the Church's faith comes from the fact that people do not remember that being Christian above all means spiritual sharing in the Body of Jesus, through which all become one in him: "there is neither Jew nor Greek, slave or freeman, male or female, for you are all one in Christ Jesus" (Galatians 3, 28). The II Vatican Council affirmed that the Church is *"in Christo veluti Sacramentum seu signum et instrumentum intimae cum Deo unionis"*—in Christ as a sacrament or sign and instrument of inward union with God. Therefore, just as we cannot do without Jesus, so we cannot do without the Church, the sole ark of salvation for all.

Let me recall, in connection with the profundity of the reality of how being a Christian differs from every other level of being, an extreme but somehow significant incident. I had gone to Assisi, and went up from there to the Carcere, together with an old English lady, with whom and with whose descendants both my family and I have kept up a long and cordial correspondence.

We came upon a peasant with his donkey, which was struggling to drag along a cart certainly bigger and heavier than it could manage. The donkey halted; it would not budge. The peasant whipped and beat it brutally. The English lady, a true animal-lover, sprang to defend it and scolded the peasant. His only reply was: "Ma, perchè non posso batterlo col bastone? Non è Cristiano!" Why can't I hit him? He's not a Christian!

He was a big, rough, ignorant man. I am sure that in these more ecumenical times he would have had more respect not only for the old English woman, but also for the donkey—at least I hope so! But in those wild days—I'm referring, you know, to twenty-eight years before the Council!—perhaps that man felt—

modo vago—what being Christian means, what the difference is between a Christian and everything else that God has created. Say what you will, this is something that some people do not know and no longer acknowledge. I hasten to add that while agreeing with the peasant's dogma, I deplore his moral theology. Donkies may have no Christian rights, but Christians have duties toward all that God has made!

Being Christian, that is, belonging to Christ, the Son of God, having God in our souls, having the well-founded hope of being able to be happy for ever in his sight, is a wonderful thing, a unique thing, which the Christian ought to know, ought to feel, ought to taste. In this time of general syncretism, of often ill understood ecumenism, it is absolutely necessary to remember and to teach what the Christian is and what his profession of being a Christian entails. A Christian is a child of God, a brother of Christ, his neighbor's servant, a voluntary slave in mankind's service.

There is a fashion, a vogue, these days for the anthropological dimension in catechesis also. This anthropology is often not only a proper regard for the psychological, sociological and environmental facts about those being catechized, but is also an effort to adapt the immutable divine doctrine to contingent states and data. It seems to me that the first thing to do is to know man, particularly since there is so much divergence among present tendencies in thought about and evaluation of man.

Some think he's some kind of angel, and pass into angelism, by trying to eliminate all sense of guilt and sin, of moral misery and spiritual infirmity from man, especially from the child.

Others think of him in purely horizontal terms, with purely temporal ends; they orientate and urge him to evaluate and accomplish himself in time and enjoy life as it goes by. This is not truth or reality. Man is a poor little being shaped from mud and subject to sin. But his nature turns him to God; by the Lord's benign gift, he is destined to enjoy God for ever. His religious life, his Christianity consequently may not be restricted to more or less philanthropical social living, but ought to be decisively and generously aimed at gaining an eternity of happiness and enjoying it.

But for the Church, man is the steward of all creation, God's image, therefore a person. Man is master of the machine and technology, not just a part of the works. Man is a pilgrim, and not only on the face of the earth; today he is a pilgrim to the moon; tomorrow he will be a pilgrim in the depths of space, then in the entire universe, illuminated by milliards of suns, but illuminated even more by that love which moves the moon, the sun, and the other stars. Man is a pilgrim in all this creation: but he is a pilgrim to eternity.

Allow me to make a brief concluding remark. The indispensable and characteristic dimension of Christian life and therefore of catechesis, is the dimension of joy. I am not sure, but this dimension of joy sometimes seems to me to have almost vanished from the Church. Joy is a victim of theological aggiornamento; it has been smothered, even buried under research, opinion polls, statistics, bibliographies, the 680 pages of the new Dutch catechism—not to mention—its 89 pages of corrigenda.

It would be disastrous if joy disappeared from catechesis. St. Augustine tells us that it is a fundamental of catechesis to teach joyfully: *"cum gaudio quis catechizet";* and he gives the reason *"multo gratius audimur cum et nos de eodem opere delectamur"*— we are listened to more willingly when we take delight in what we are saying. We ought not only give but also taste and delight in what we are communicating. Here is the whole secret and power of teaching religion; it is loving what we want to say so deeply and vitally in ourselves that we can exult and delight in it and so, by the Lord's grace, teach and convey it to others.

III
Faith and the Theologies

In 1967, our Holy Father, Pope Paul, called for a full year of meditation on the nature of faith.

All over the Catholic world truly Christian communities (dioceses, parishes and families, each in its own way "the Church in miniature") were asked to plan appropriate ways and means of promoting within their communities of spiritual life and of supernatural love that unity and fidelity in the faith which alone can make them healthy cells of the total body of the Church.

The faithful, laymen and clergy, were especially invited to repeat frequently the Credo so long beloved in the Catholic tradition and to renew the simple Act of Faith that we learned among the prayers of childhood. No subsequent growth in theological knowledge or religious sophistication has brought us substantially beyond these—the Credo and the Act of Faith—so far as pertains to the faith which saves, the faith which is "the substance of things to be hoped for."

This focus on faith has not come a bit too soon; its importance cannot possibly be exaggerated.

Sometimes it is said that the crisis of our moment in the history of the Church is one of faith. This may ultimately turn out to be true. Many of us think that all mankind, fascinated by the bewitchery of the new technology and satiated by the materialistic affluence of our new society, is headed for a winter of unbelief, of denial of the Christian faith and rejection of the law of Christ. Such a winter was foretold by the English convert, Cardinal Newman, by the Russian Orthodox Vladimir Soloviev, and by many sensitive, prophetic spirits among the French, the Italians and the Germans in the last century, to speak only of these. It was preparation for this winter (and for the eventual new spring of Christian faith) which prompted (one thinks) the canny Pope John to call the Ecumenical Council.

But the present religious turbulence may not yet be so profound as a crisis in faith. It does, however, touch on corollaries of the faith and even threatens it. There is probably a crisis in hope, especially, perhaps, in areas of personal and social life where moral idealism increasingly calls for heroism in the face of the compromises, personal and social, demanded of the Christian. Certainly there is a crisis in theology—but theology is *not* the faith and all the "theologies" combined do not add up to the faith. Perhaps one reason there is some passing confusion and contradiction in the *household of the faith* is that we have had, with all our other explosions, an explosion of writers, lecturers and columnists.

It is this last theme that I wish to emphasize, for "theologies" are influenced by human conditionings (cultural, political, subjective) but the faith is from God and its content is from His Revelation through Christ Jesus.

It is quite possible to be adept in theological speculation and yet be quite devoid of faith. We have had widely publicized evidence recently that men could write, with scholarly competence and persuasive erudition, theological commentaries on the faith while themselves unable to make or persevere in the personal act of faith which is the heart of the matter. Few men could expound with greater lucidity or poetic grace the Christian theology of the Trinity, the Incarnation and certain concepts of Mariology than could a gifted Spanish-American philosopher of whom I think with affectionate prayer whenever I read of certain contemporary defectors from the *faith,* some of whom continue to teach *theology.* This philosopher (Santayana) wrote with seductive beauty of theological concepts dear to us believers, but he had no *faith* (or said he had none), any more than professors of classical mythology or ancient pagan history believe the "theologies" of the ancient world of the Age of Fable.

Conversely, as millions have understood with Louis Pasteur, the French scientist, it is possible (even common, though not ideal) to have the *faith* that justifies and saves even though one be totally innocent of theology in any academic or "scientific" sense.

The first point to be kept clear in the present religious and spiritual crisis is that there is a sharp distinction between the *faith* and "the theologies," between *belief* and theological *speculation*. The distinction is as real and as wide as the distinction between Jesus Christ, the source and object of Christian faith, and *any* theologian, even one whose opinions, insights or speculations may have won for him a school of admirers, a group of partisans or a large reading public. Theologians and their schools of thought are the objects of interest, criticism, often admiration or gratitude for the lines of thought that they open up; but Jesus Christ, and the Church as His appointed Voice, can alone be the object of faith.

Much of the present crisis in religion is perhaps due to confusions arising from failure to keep clear these distinctions between "the theologies" and "the faith." The exciting years of the Council experience, years ultimately rich in spiritual profit even as the Council itself can only be seen as providential, have stimulated minds and dizzied some imaginations with the theoretical speculations, reasonings, wit, wisdom, subtlety and occasional abberations (omnis homo mendax) of scores of theologians who suddenly became popular lecturers, authors of best sellers or TV personalities. We have heard, with varied reactions and profit, the widely different voices of the theologians, not to mention theologizers; their role in the thought-life of the Church and the culture of the general community is great, at times fortunately colossal, usually positive, occasionally confusing and sometimes potentially calamitous.

Theologians are men: the thoughts of men are many and divided. Theological theories set forth aspects, elements, corollaries of the faith. They provide reasonings about the faith. But theologians are not *sources of faith* nor are their *speculations* the *object* of faith.

Jesus Christ is God. The thought of God is one and unites; God's revelations are the object of faith. His Church authoritatively sets forth God's revelation. The Church is not a forum nor a school of theologians and theologies, though she is greatly helped by these in the total work of explaining the faith that she is called to do. The Church is the channel through which God's revelation reaches men, including theologians, so that believers may enjoy the privilege of reflecting on the content of revelation, as do theologians, but may also, and above all else, *live* in the light of the revelation—as must all the faithful, including the theologians. Only what the Church teaches authoritatively as the mind and the will of Christ the Lord is the object of faith; all the theologies, even those which most she welcomes as helpful in understanding the faith or blesses as most consistent with the content of faith are secondary and marginal, related to the faith, perhaps, but not to be confused with it.

The crisis disturbing so many in our generation derives from the fact that such a confusion has taken place. Suddenly caught up in the intricacies and fascinations of theologies, people have supposed the faith to be at issue in the speculations that they have found so exciting. And so it is well to recall, as should be obvious, that the theologians we hold in admiration or hold in disdain, whether they be Dutch, Belgian, French, German, Spanish, Italian or American; whether they be among the dead, like Newman, Franzelin, Teilhard de Chardin, Scotus, Bonaventure, Aquinas (or among the living like McCormick, Cox, Altizer and Who Not?) may be—normally are—authentic *scholars,* but they are also fallible *men.* Some are professional theologians of measurable competence and degrees of insight, perhaps (as we have discreetly suggested) even degrees also of faith. In any case, they are the objects of such attention, gratitude and agreement as the critical, intelligent listener or reader may deem them to deserve. It is entirely different, as *theologians would themselves be the first to confess,* with Jesus Christ and the authentic teaching Voice of His Church. Christ and what God teaches through the channels of revelation committed to the care and judgment of the *magisterium* in the Church, are the objects of our faith.

The various "theologies" may be freely examined, freely espoused, some freely rejected; not so with the faith as such. Here, as Pope Paul has recently pointed out, freedom takes on other formalities so far as the Christian is concerned. Although we are free (psychologically, though not equally so morally) to accept the faith of Jesus Christ or not ("Faith is free in the act which expresses it") we are not free in the formulation of the content of the faith. We are not free to pick and choose among the articles of faith, as we would be to choose critically among the contentions of the theologians. The faith involves a total, unqualified commitment to God in His Christ, echoed authentically through His Church. The faith is an integral response, "the one faith" willed by Christ and transmitted by the Apostles. It may be weak; it may be faltering; it may be (often is) excruciating in its obscurity ("I believe, O Lord, help thou my unbelief!"), but it is a total commitment that the Christian can give to no man, to no theological opinion and, therefore, to no theologian. Only of Jesus can we say, with St. Paul: Scio cui credidi. Of theologians we can only say: Scio quid dicit—sed quis et qualis est, solus Deus scit. (I only know what he says. Who really knows him, except God!)

Any crisis in the Church arising from confusions among theologians and rival commitments to theological parties or personalities is no new thing. Saint Paul was confronted in the Church at Corinth with a situation which seems precisely parallel to the confusions which so challenge Pope Paul and all others who cherish the faith as the foundation of Christian hope and the fountainhead of divine charity. Pope Paul, pleading for a Year of Faith, might easily substitute contemporary names for those which Saint Paul used in his letter to the Corinthians when partisan "theologies" and conflicting personalities threatened the unity of the faith among the people:

"I appeal to you, brethren, by the name of Our Lord Jesus Christ, that all of you agree and that there be no dissensions among you, but that you be united in the same mind and the same judgment. For it has been reported to me by Chloe's people that there is quarreling among you, my brethren. What I mean is that each of you says, 'I belong to Paul,' or 'I belong to Apollos,' or 'I belong to Cephas,' or 'I belong to Christ.' Is Christ divided? Was Paul crucified for you? Or were you baptized in the name of Paul?" (I Corinthians 1: 10-13).

Clearly this is an old story—and a new one. Theological debate, lively and fruitful, is indispensable to religious progress and to renewal of Christian life, thought and values; but the loving service of the faith and unqualified adherence to the univocal teaching of the Church concerning the undivided Christ, who alone was crucified for us and to whom alone we were committed by faith at Baptism—these are the basic, the essential, the enduring needs, demands, joys of the Christian creed and code.

That is why we who dearly love freedom, cherish faith even more passionately. That is why we who rejoice in the renewal of theological studies in and around the Second Vatican Council, welcomed not less the "Year of Faith" by which Pope Paul hoped to make secure the good coming out of the Council and fortify that authentic teaching of the Church without which theological discussions and speculations become unsubstantial and fanciful. For "the theologies" without authentic faith speedily become like to the fragile writings of so many romanticists and aesthetes who speak nostalgically, but unprofitably of the beauty of a faith that they no longer *believe* as true or *live* as good and essential to salvation.

For faith is always something *lived,* commitment of the total person, unto death itself. Hear St. Paul:

"By faith Abel offered to God a more acceptable sacrifice than

Cain through which he received approval as righteous, God bearing witness by accepting his gifts; he died but through his faith he is still speaking. By faith Enoch was taken up so that he should not see death; and he was not found, because God had taken him. Now before he was taken he was attested as having pleased God. And without faith it is impossible to please him. For whoever would draw near to God must believe that He exists and that He rewards those who seek Him. By faith Noah, being warned by God concerning events as yet unseen, took heed and constructed an ark for the saving of his household; by this he condemned the world and became an heir of the righteousness which comes by faith.

"By faith Abraham obeyed when he was called to go out to a place which he was to receive as an inheritance and he went out, not knowing where he was to go. . . .

"These all died in faith, not having received what was promised, but having seen it and greeted it from afar, and having acknowledged that they were strangers and exiles on the earth. For people who speak thus make it clear that they are seeking a homeland. . . .

"By faith Moses, when he was born was hid for three months by his parents, because they saw that the child was beautiful; and they were not afraid of the king's edict. By faith Moses, when he was grown up, refused to be called the son of Pharoh's daughter, choosing rather to share ill-treatment with the people of God than to enjoy the fleeting pleasures of sin. . . . By faith he left Egypt, not being afraid of the anger of the king; for he endured as seeing Him who is invisible. By faith he kept the Passover and sprinkled the blood so that the Destroyer of the first-born might not touch them.

"By faith the people crossed the Red Sea as if on dry land; but the Egyptians, when they attempted to do the same, were drowned. . . .

"And what more shall I say? For time would fail me to tell of

Gideon, Barak, Samson, Jephthan, of David and Samuel and the prophets—who through faith conquered kingdoms, enforced justice, received promises, stopped the mouths of lions, quenched raging fire, escaped the edge of the sword, won strength out of weakness, became mighty in war, put foreign armies to flight. Women received their dead by resurrection. Some were tortured, refusing to accept release, that they might rise again to a better life. Others suffered mocking and scourging, and even chains and imprisonment. They were stoned, they were sawn in two, they were killed with the sword; they went about in skins of sheep and goats, destitute, afflicted, ill treated—of whom the world was not worthy—wandering over deserts and mountains, and in dens and caves of the earth. . . .

"Therefore, since we are surrounded by so great a cloud of witnesses, let us lay aside every weight, and sin which clings so closely, and let us run with perseverance the race that is set before us, looking to Jesus the pioneer and perfecter of our faith, who for the joy that was set before Him endured the cross, despising the shame, and is seated at the right hand of the throne of God." (Hebrews 11: 4-8, 10, 13-14, 23-25, 27-29, 32-38; 12, 1-2).

Such is the faith! But theology, and especially "the theologies," on the other hand, is a question of systems of thought, human reasonings. It may be sublime; it may be beautiful; it may shed light on the faith and help vivify it—but it may also become either ossified or rarified and, in either case, a substitute for faith. "The theologies" may make divine truths merely human, whereas the faith makes even human things somehow divine, eternal like God Himself!

IV
The Point of
Contemporary Catechetics

Six years after the end of Vatican Council II, there have begun to emerge the fruits of the pastoral renewal promised by that Council. But at the same time there are also emerging ever more clearly the problems and the difficulties attached to developng Christian pastoral action in a secularized and desacralized world, particularly in the field of the ministry of the Word of God.

In the Scriptural phrase, the wheat, the harvest of the Council, is rich and abundant, but some enemies, not all outside the Church, have sown cockle in the midst of the wheat. Cardinal Heenan recently underlined the consequent mutual recrimination, scandalous disunity, promotion of intolerance and, in particular, *"the contemporary outburst of sectarianism in the field of catechetics"* which have been the result of this evil. The English Cardinal made a most charitable defence of the honest intent and loving faith of many teachers of catechism unjustly attacked for "subversion" of the faith simply because they perceive that the *new methods* are as necessary in religious as in secular education. Despite the many and grave errors which he sees as indubitably present in the "new catechetics," he asserts that these will be corrected in due time. *Magna est veritas et praevalebit*. But, he insists, quite rightly, that despite the imperfections of their catechetics, it is wrong, unjust, uncharitable to condemn teachers who sincerely seek to lead people, above all youth, to the Lord. His discourse is a balanced criticism of the *mood* of contemporary controversy over catechetics. (*The Tablet,* London; May 22, 1971).

More positive and helpful, perhaps, are the observations

concerning the *content* or *premises* of contemporary catechetcs made a few months ago by the Auxiliary Bishop of Chicago, Bishop William E. McManus. He strongly criticized "the tendency to take *sociology* rather than *theology* as the staring point for religious education." He said that teachers of Christian Doctrine should *"make religion what it should be, not just reflect what it is in our society."*

In a spirited discourse, rich with insights into the sociological threat to religious faith, Bishop McManus agreed that "theological emphasis should not ignore the need for contemporary teaching methods nor deny the need to adapt catechetics to the emotional and psychological development of the child. But the starting point of catechetics must be the data of revelation found in the Bible, the self-consciousness and the tradition of the Church through the ages."

Citing Pope Paul's Palm Sunday homily of this year, Bishop McManus spoke on the nature of Christianity and on the obligation of the bishop to make sure that the teaching of Christianity is in competent hands. He said, "Christianity is a logical, coherent response of truly free and faithful men. Youth today are called from a passive and routine, to an active and dynamic Christianity; from a timid and inept, to a militant and courageous faith; from an individual private life, to one of community and fellowship; from indifference and insensibility, to openness and care for others. We fail them if our outlook is not creative and constructive. We cannot be without adequate funds, the best of personnel."

Then Bishop McManus added a wry observation: "The bishop traditionally employed a full-time master of ceremonies to make sure he did not *fall on his face* in the sanctuary. It's time he hired true professionals to make sure he doesn't *fall on his face* in much more important matters."

Well, maybe! But there are those of us who believe that *professionalism,* despite all its virtue, can ruin religion more quickly than *sin*—at least if the sinners have contrite and humble hearts!

Personally, I would give top priority to the choice by the bishop of a good father-confessor to examine him on how he fulfills the duties of his state in life, beginning with the teaching of the faith.

However, one must agree with an analysis of our contemporary problem of catechesis so well stated and so honest. Nonetheless, one wonders if, while being correct in asking that Christian Doctrine *not* begin with *sociology*, Bishop McManus has not attached a little too much importance to the "professionals" of a discipline which, in the last analysis, also seeks to be, like *sociology*, an autonomous science, namely, *theology*. I wonder if it would not be more exact and more proper to say that the study of religion, certainly of Christian Doctrine, should begin with the *faith* and with the creation of all that spiritual and moral climate, as well as intellectual openness, in which the *faith* can flourish, while using theology and, in its own way, sociology, as *aids,* means of clarification, collaborators, even as other sciences like anthropology and psychology, certainly the arts of sciences of mass communications—but with the *faith* first and foremost, not *theology* nor sociology. The plain fact is that theology is *not* the faith; there are a hundred theologies, good and bad, and indifferent; there is only *one faith.*

Permit me to pause for comment on the special importance of the place of audio-visual techniques in modern catechetics. Our main problem is that there seems to be some misunderstanding about the relation of communications to catechetics. People have not yet realized sufficiently that in an electronic world we have passed from the concept of "visual aids" to the concept of the "Visual Message."

Whether we like it or not, it is the audio-visual message that is forming modern man, for better or worse, and we believe that it is the goal of catechetics to illuminate this audio-visual message with the light of the Gospel. In Mexico, for example, a Center for the service of all Latin America is in preparation; it is late, but it is providential. It is the great, indispensable instrument for future evangelization.

Even here, however, not so much "professionals" are needed to teach the faith; the great need is for committed, ardent, credible, *believers*—not mere scientists, not mere technicians—who, in one way or another, have seen the Lord Jesus, have had their lives transformed by His power, and, therefore, advance as their reason for being heard, not their academic degrees, their certificate or their acceditation, but the title that the Apostles claimed for themselves: We cannot do other than speak *of those things that we have seen and heard* (Acts 4, 20).

Today we are facing some serious problems concerning the pastoral renewal of the Church, problems that directly or indirectly interest the catechetical sector of the Church.

Some of these problems are inevitable; others are even desirable, as is the anvil on which the artisan hammers out the desired model. Some of them involve cultural, even political and cultural elements which create a credibility gap for the community of faith, a gap not bridged by a multiplication of "theologies," the multiplicity of which, praiseworthy in itself, can reach a point where it obscures that unity of the faith which is, in fact, the strongest argument for its divine origin. *The thoughts of men are many and divide: the thought of God is one and unites.* "Theologies" are the thoughts of men, thoughts about divine truths, to be sure, and by intent and usual effect these are means to the clarificaion and enriching of the faith. But "theologies" are conditioned by human cultures, temperaments, understandings and even prejudices; they are the objects of reason and critical intelligence. Faith, on the other hand, is made possible by grace; it is a total personal response to the Living God speaking through His Incarnate Son and His Church.

It would be dishonest to deny that one of the problems confronting the Church today is the fact that a mistaken interpretation of Vatican Council II and of the Ecumenical Movement has led superficial Catholics to forget that the Catholic Church is a "Missionary Church" which seeks, without shame or apology, to bring all men into visible unity within that single fold, under a single Shepherd, concerning which Jesus was so explicit, so uncompromising and so clear.

What has become of the missionary spirit? What has become of the generous, loving desire to *share* the *faith,* not only dollars, shirts and food. These, certainly, we are commanded to share—to sacrifice to the point of "giving all," as Jesus told the rich young man—but not more nor less than we are bound to go to the ends of the earth to make disciples of all through the missionary apostolate; to be active, through the aposolate of conversions, in our neighborhoods, our own families, our own social and professional circles, seeking with unfeigned charity, *in opere et veritate,* conversions to Christ in His Church. The day of the apostle has not passed. It is not less true in the post-Conciliar world than it was in the Apostolic Age, indeed from the very beginning, that "not by bread alone does man live, but by every word that proceeds from the mouth of God." Other mouths have important lessons to teach us on how to implement our moral duties, personal and social. We must listen to them all, but not to the exclusion of the voice of God proclaiming the faith that demands good works, or else the good works are speedily smothered under indifference and callousness.

Our 1971 Congress responds to the need for a fraternal exchange of experiences and of opinions concerning the subject of catechetics at the level of responsibility both of people who are active in the field and of those whom long studies have made experts in this material. Precisely at this moment in which some of the more serious arguments have ended or been allayed there exists a better disposition of soul to listen and to be listened to.

Catechetics is a reality that has been present in the Church from her earliest days, although the term *catechetics* took on its specific meaning only at the end of the II Century, on the occasion of the organization of the catechumenate. (Cfr. A. TURCK. *"Catéchein et Catechesis chez les premiers Pères."* In Rev. ScPhTh. 47, 1963, 361-372).

In fact, in early Christian preaching—which could be considered in some way as a pattern of the discussions which developed later—there exist unquestionably two distinct phases: the phase of *kerygma* or evangelization properly so called, characterized by the announcement of the Resurrection of Christ, of God's approval of Him and of the salvation of all men through Jesus, and the phase of *instruction* and *further exhortation* to the converts in terms of the new life that they should lead (Acts 2, 40 ff.). It is precisely in this second phase that catechetics is placed in its fundamental dimension. In addition, the study of the baptismal rite of the Church of the first two centuries seems to point to the conclusion that the concern of pastors in that period concentrated—besides evangelization properly so called—on the instruction to be given to the new converts and on their Christian formation, that is to say on catechetics. In this concern will be found the basic reason for the catechumenate. This can't be other that the institutionalization, actualized at the beginning of the II century, of those instructions or catechising of the new converts, given before and after baptism, initially by those who, at the forefront of the Christian community, were the guarantors (the godparents) of the authenticity of their conversion, and also, later, by authorized catechists and by the pastors of the community themselves. (Cfr. G. GROPPO. "Omilia e catechesi." In *Rivista Liturgica,* 57, 1970, 563-675).

We cannot fail to recall on this point the authoritative statement of Pope John XXIII of holy memory. Speaking to Lenten preachers of Rome on February 22, 1962, he said:

"Catechism is the constant preoccupation of the Church.

"In diocesan synods as well as in provincial and regional councils of the Middle Ages and above all in ecumenical councils this solicitude takes forms, varied according to the demands and the conditions of the times, but basically the same, that is, to break the bread of truth into simple and intelligible pieces that can be grasped and meditated upon and passed on in the family as a precious heritage."

We can recall the wise dispositions of the Council of Trent (Sess. XXIV, *De reformatione,* can. 4, 7) and other documents of the Holy See which throw light on the Church's interest in finding ever more apt solutions to the catechetical problem. But we will limit ourselves to recalling only a few instances closer to us: the innumerable catechetical references made by St. Pius X (more than 21 documents dealing directly with catechetics, among which is the important encyclical *Acerbo nimis* of April 15, 1905) and the decree of Pius XI, *Provido Sane,* January 12, 1935, by which all catechetical activity was revitalized on a world-wide basis through the institution of *Diocesan Catechetical Offices.*

Pope Pius XII gave a truly great stimulus to catechetics above all through his example: his marvellous talks to all classes of people are a wonderful catechetical summary, an authoritative interpretation of reality in human problems under the light of the Gospel. (Cfr. G. FRUMENTO. "La catechesi nei documenti della Santa Sede." Roma. Edizioni Paoline. 1965).

One might perhaps wonder at the fact that Vatican Council II did not dedicate a document specifically to the theme of catechesis. But if we would wish to gather from the different Conciliar documents all the texts that implicitly or explicitly treat the subject of catechetics and to arrange them in logical order, we would be surprised to find a real summary of catechetics and a kind of Conciliar catechetical directory, so great is the mass of texts of unexpected doctrinal richness that reveal a basic homogeneousness.

We limit ourselves to recalling but a few of the principal declarations.

The Council has clearly affirmed the importance of catechetics in the whole apostolate of the Church; not only that, but it has even affirmed that among the duties of bishops in regard to announcing the word of God, catechetics together with liturgical preaching occupies the first place: "They should also strive to use the various means at hand today for making Christian doctrine known: namely, first of all, preaching and catechetical instruction which always hold pride of place . . . " (CD. 13).

In a paragraph found in the Decree on the Pastoral Office of Bishops, which truly provides a program for the renewal of catechetics, the nature, purpose and task of catechetics are defined: "Catechetical training is intended to make men's faith become living, conscious, and active, through the light of instruction. Bishops should see to it that such training be painstakingly given to children, adolescents, young adults, and even grownups. In this instruction a proper sequence should be observed as well as a method conformed to the matter that is being treated and to the natural disposition, ability, age and circumstances of life of the listener. Finally, they should see to it that this instruction be based on sacred Scripture, tradition, the liturgy, the teaching authority, and life of the Church.

"Much more they should take care that catechists be properly trained for their task, so that they will be thoroughly acquainted with the doctrine of the Church and will have both a theoretical knowledge of the laws of psychology and of pedagogical methods.

"Bishops should also strive to reestablish, or better adapt the instruction of adult catechumens" (CD. 14).

As we can see, although it is brief, the passage has not left out anything: catechetics of adults and the catechumenate, sources of doctrine and the need for the anthropological sciences for an adequate preparation of the catechists.

The educational aspect of catechetics is spotlighted in the Council's Declaration on Christian Education:

"In discharging her educative function, the Church is concerned with all appropriate means to that end. But she is particularly concerned with the means which are proper to herself, of which catechetical training is foremost. Such instruction gives clarity and vigor to the faith, nourishes a life lived according to the spirit of Christ, leads to a knowing and active participation in the liturgical mystery, and inspires apostolic action" (GE. 4).

The Council has understood, however, that a true renewal of catechetics must be the fruit of appropriate study, made on an international level by experts and pastors of souls, and, therefore, at the end of the Decree on the Pastoral Office of the Bishops, it insists that there be published general pastoral directories, among which a catechetical directory is explicitly mentioned:

"This Sacred Synod also prescribes that general directories be drawn up concerning the care of souls, for the use of both bishops and pastors. . . . There should also be prepared individual directories concerning the pastoral care of special groups of the faithful. . . . Another directory should be composed with respect to the catechetical instruction of the Christian people, and should deal with the fundamental principles of such instruction, its arrangement and the composition of books on the subject . . . " (CD. 44). (Cfr. G. M. MEDICA. "La catechesi nei documenti del Vaticano II," in: Catechesi, 35 1966, n. 310, pp. 1-13; n. 314, pp. 1-23).

Vatican II's promise of a general catechetical directory constituted a special obligation for the then Sacred Congregation of the Council, now called the Sacred Congregation for the Clergy, an obligation that was carried out with a deep sense of responsibility.

The need for a General Catechetical Directory can be considered the natural result of an examination of conscience by both theologians and pastors concerning the ministerial function of the ecclesial community with relation to the word of God. There was felt on many sides the need for renewal in the work of announcing the word of God. Evangelization, catechetics, liturgical preaching, all had an impact on listeners, both believing and non-believing, that they seem to have lost. It was felt more or less clearly that such a renewal should arise from the context of a general renewal of the whole pastoral action of the Church. Only within the reality of joint pastoral action, carefully designed according to the needs of contemporary man, can traditional catechetics find its way, can it be rejuvenated and bear abundant fruit.

All this was deeply felt by those responsible for catechetics in the Sacred Congregation for the Clergy and inspired the commission that worked to compile the General Directory.

It is our intention now to point out briefly what are today, in our view, the problems and the basic directions of contemporary catechetics on the world level, indicating at the same time how the General Directory has tried to take account of them.

Everyone knows that the contemporary catechetical movement has arisen as a reply to a situation that became more and more unacceptable: that is, a catechetics that was exaggeratedly idealistic and abstract, that concentrated on an expression of a catechetical formula, that ignored or did not take sufficient account of the assimilative capacity of children and youth; a catechetics isolated from the general context of pastoral activity in the Church and did not reach, or reached in an inadequate manner, the world of adults. Seventy years of efforts and of reflection have brought about notable progress in the elimination of these defects in catechetics; nevertheless the work to be done is still great; in all probability, it will never end, because life does not stop changing.

The development of the catechetical movement has passed through three principal periods. We began with the need for renewing the *method* of religious, scholastic and parochial instruction, applying to catechetics the conclusions affirmed ever more forcefully by contemporary pedagogy and the art of teaching: the inductive method, the principle of activity, the utilization of modern teaching aids, etc.

The *kerygmatic* period, began a little before the Second World War and developed immediately after; the multiple ferments of renewal that appeared in that period in the field of theology, focused the attention of the catechetical movement on the problems of the content of catechetics, on the attempt to reach a more kerygmaic exposition of the Christian message, not only, but also, to offer in this way a solution to the grave problems posited by contemporary society. From this point on there is a notable improvement in catechisms and in texts of religious Instruction which are characterized by a large biblical and liturgical content.

At the same time there emerges from deep within the catechetical movement the need for a better preparation of those responsible for catechetics on all levels: the originality of the catechetical function demands a specific preparation (which theological studies often do not give), which can be achieved only through an adequate pedagogical and pastoral formation. From this need there have emerged and have been approved in different parts of the world higher institutes of catechetics and up-dating courses for catechetical workers themselves.

The post-Conciliar period has seen the problems of catechetics increase: we find ourselves faced by a critical situation characterized by uncertainty and by a feverish search for new solutions.

A sense of bewilderment appears to be finding its way into not a few of the experts on catechetical problems. The titles of recent publications bear this out: "La catechesi contestata" (Colomb); "La contestazione nella catechesi" (Rica); "Abbandono la catechesi" (Babin); "La crisi della moneta spicciola in teologia e in catechesi" (Le Du); "Dove va la catechesi" (Varela), etc. Everything appears to be thrown into controversy: method, structure, catechetical content, those to be catechized and the catechetical workers themselves, the presence of catechists in the school, etc. And this series of problems is all the more weighty because it is not isolated, but is part of the whole, general pastoral problem which has beset the post-Conciliar Church. We are asked about the usefulness of the traditional structures of the Church's pastoral activity, about the relation between the clergy and the laity, between the Church and the world, about the reason for preaching to the world today, about the purpose of administering baptism to babies, about the function of the Sacrament of Penance, etc. In a word, the catechetical field today appears to be invaded more than ever before by profound, innovating forces, which, if, on the one hand are a source of rejoicing because they show forth the vitality of the post-Conciliar Church, on the other hand, they leave us perplexed concerning their opportuneness and concerning their fidelity to the Christian message.

All the same, there is observable in this whole movement, which at first glance appears a bit chaotic, some examples and some indication of a valid core. It is our purpose now briefly to underline some of these positive aspects.

a) *Catechetics must aim toward the formation of an adult faith, not only in the individual, but also in the Christian community.*

There is a movement today to overcome once and for all the catechetical infantilism that regards catechetics as an activity aimed principally at youngsters and children. Conceiving catechetics as the second step in Christian preaching, catechetics should be considered the perfection of the kerygma; its scope is to bring to maturity that faith which the first announcement of the Good News has awakened. Consequently, catechetics ought to follow man all through life right into his human maturity, and in the adult man it reaches its peak.

There is also an effort made today to overcome that kind of individualism which overlooks the group as such in order to care for the religious development only of individuals. Maturity in faith ought to come about, whether on the level of the individual or on the level of the groups that comprise the ecclesial community, in such a way that this community can become an adult community— not of "individuals" but of "*persons.*"

61

All this had led to a basic position, clearly expressed in the Directory: affirmation of the irreplaceable importance of adult catechetics, and not only that, but the characterizing of adult catechetics as the principal form of catechetics; "it is to be remembered that adult catechetics . . . is to be considered the principal form of catechetics; toward which all the other forms, not thereby less necessary, are ordered . . . " (n. 20).

Catechetics should not lead to infantilism in the faith, to religious passivity, to the lack of a critical sense, to the inability to dialogue with non-Catholics, etc.; on the contrary it ought to be the promotion agent of an adult faith on the personal level and on the level of community, a faith that is thus well founded, integrated, serious, open, in a word, a faith of men matured in Christianity.

b) *Catechetics ought to lead to an integration between faith and life.*

By its very purpose, catechetics ought to be able to transmit a message, which is that of Christ, possessed, lived and vitally communicated by the Church, in such a way that it does not appear detached from the real life in which adults and youth are immersed: family, friendship, study, work, aspirations, sickness, etc. The word of God that the catechist announces ought to appear as an illumination of life which comes from on high, as a reply to the most serious problems and to the real pleas for help of the man of today. From this, prospective "human" themes (love, war, social justice, peace, personal formation, etc.) do not pertain to catechetics only as examples used for pedagogic purposes, but they pertain as *content,* which the Word of God must illuminate. (Cfr. D.C.G., nn. 9, 26, 45).

From this point of view one can speak of a *liberating catechetics.* Catechetics, therefore, ought to help persons and Christian communities to become conscious of the *socio-political dimension of the faith* in a world where there is an ever growing awareness of the duty of all to strive for the building up of a world and a society that is more human, not only on the level of individual nations but also on an international basis. Politics, in the best sense of the word, has become a basic dimension of the life of every conscientious and responsible man: on it depends the very future of humanity. Catechetics not only should not deter a Christian from responsible efforts to transform society but should help him to carry out that transformation, enlightening him about the meaning of the true liberation of man, showing how illusory is a liberation that is purely economic and cultural, unaccompanied by a spiritual liberation from sin and selfishness. Precisely for this reason catechetics should interest itself above all and with particular preference in the poor and in those on the margins of society, but without yielding to the temptation to present the message of Christ as a merely social message. Catechetics should never become a promotor of violent revolution, simply because in this way it would betray the Word of Christ (Cfr. DCG, nn. 9, 29, 49).

Finally, it is always in this sense that catechetics must avoid presenting a sort of dualistic religion, a religiosity that removes man from earthly concerns which pertain to the divine plan of the total redemption of man; nor should catechetics separate personal faith from what we call *sentire cum Ecclesia*. We are talking about not separating God and man, body and spirit, nature and supernature, human development and the salvation of the soul, while at the same time not confusing these concepts.

c) *Catechetics must be placed within the pastoral action of the Church.*

Students of catechetical pastoral action are agreed that any catechetical activity that is isolated from the ecclesial context in which it exists is destined to be inefficacious. Not parochial catechetics, catechetics in schools, family instruction, conferences for special groups of believers nor any other kind of catechetics can be effective by itself. Consequently it is unthinkable that catechetical activity be developed without connection and collaboration with other ecclesial activity. It is to be especially underlined that it is necessary that every catechetical activity be related to a concrete community of the faithful who live their faith effectively. All this is considered in the DCG, particularly in the last section which is dedicated to the organization of catechetics on the general plane of joint pastoral action.

d) Ecumenical dimension of catechetics

Keeping in mind that adult catechetics represents the principal form of catechetics, this type of catechetics should be the promotor of great human understanding and effective dialogue among all men. This should be accomplished without falling into irenics that are superficial and contrary to truth. However, catechetics ought to make Christians and the Christian community emerge from behind unnatural barriers, from forms of ghetto. This vision ought to inspire an ecumenical dimension and missionary zeal in the catechist, promoting, of course, respect for the religious liberty of the non-believer, while affirming without hiding his own conviction of the truth of Catholicism (Cfr. DCG, nn. 27, 28. E. ALBERICH. *Orientamenti della catechesi,* "Quaderni di Pedagogia Catechistica," A. 1 Torino, L.C.D. 1971, pp. 168).

With these points of view, the General Directory intends to take its place in a progressive balanced way within the contemporaneous catechetical movement. We are not ignorant, however, of the problems still unresolved, or resolved according to views that leave us perplexed. This is precisely the reason that the Congress has come about: for a serene discussion and a sincere exchange of views directed toward a better carrying out of the ministry of the Word in catechetics.

I sometimes fear that one of the temporary causalities of the post-Conciliar mood of contestation, doubt, review of old attitudes and old practices, has been the virtue of *joy.* A dismal, apprehensive, melancholic-depressed absence of *joy, spontaneous and sin-*

cere, characterizes so many aspects of our religious life at the moment.

It is fashionable to pretend that we Catholics used to go to Mass out of a sense of duty, rigorous, obedient and lackluster; the fact is that most of us do not remember things that way at all. We remember the Masses of childhood and youth with *joy.* It may well be, that a refreshed sense of Christian community, which the new liturgy aspires to develop among us in an age more conscious of community, it is said, and certainly more collectivist in its tendencies, will ultimately develop among us its characteristic spirit of Christian *joy.* But it is no exaggeration to say that it has not yet done so, certainly not in any degree that cancels out the memory of the joy of the Mass as it was sung and celebrated by our forefathers.

Pardon any trace of triumphalism and also the optimism of faith—I believe, O Lord, help Thou my *unbelief*—but the plain fact is that authentic faith is always humble, to be sure, because we bear it in fragile vessels, but it is also always somehow "triumphalistic" because faith is always a victory. By faith we overcome ourselves. By faith we have overcome the world *in* and *with* and *through* Jesus Christ. We have overcome death in and with the Risen Christ. We have overcome *ourselves* by the teaching of His Gospel and, therefore, we should heed His joyful cry: *Rejoice,* for I have overcome the world! Rejoice! again I say to you, rejoice!— as St. Paul never wearied of repeating to those whom he catechized. Be strong in the faith, be militant in the Faith, be persevering in the faith—but as the condition of all these other qualities, be *glad* in the faith, *rejoice* in the faith. Let your faith be the source of your joy and your joy be the proof of your faith. This must be the spirit of all catechesis!

We must not permit catechesis—the simple direct study of the faith, its content, its motives, its effects—to give way to the pedestrian study of comparative religion or to desperate efforts to spell out a complicated "Theology of Hope"—nineteen centuries

65

after the Resurrection; a "Theology of Love"—nineteen centuries after the Crucifixion; a "Theology of Community"—nineteen centuries after the Last Supper, Pentecost, and the promise of Jesus that where two or three are gathered in His Name, there He is in the midst of them.

The catechesis needed today is that which is set forth in St. Luke's Gospel, chapter 24, where is described the two melancholy, discouraged, confused disciples in flight from Jerusalem to Emmaus. Suddenly Jesus stood beside them and said: "What are these conversations you are having among you, and are sad?". They replied: "We expected so many wonderful *changes* and now we are sad!". *Sperabamus! Sperabamus!* They were precisely like some—but by no means *all*—post-Council Catholics! We had hope . . . but no longer!

What did Jesus do? He did not give a course in theology. He did not give them a *saggio* in exegesis. He did not have a "dialogue" or a symposium on the *problemi scottanti del momento*. He did not explain their depression of spirit in sociological or psychological terms. *He gave them a lesson in catechetics.* He recalled not theories, not speculations—but *facts of doctrine— dogmas of faith*: how Jesus was obliged to suffer and to die, so He and they could enter into glory. And *their hearts* burned with love—and faith—and they ran back to Jerusalem with joy.

We must not permit the *faith* to be buried alive under *rival theologies;* we must not permit the response to Christ and to God, that is the essence of Faith, to be smothered in the effort to make sense out of the claims and contentions of this new race which has taken the place of preachers, catechists, heralds of the Word, witnesses to Christ, apostles of the Son of God, ambassadors of the Absolute, the strictly contemporary little group who call themselves *"professional theologians,"* as other are "professional bonesetters," professional political theorists, professional tax experts, professional investment consultors, or professional therapists.

The tradition of theologians in all the Christian Churches is a rich tradition and a proud one, even a charismatic and prophetic tradition. But theologians hitherto thought of themselves, above all, as priests or other believers eager to clarify, explain, increase our knowledge of what *Jesus* said, not what *they* think. They were not given to arid speculation; the Saint whom the present *gurus* accuse of having been the most arid of past theologians, St. Thomas Aquinas, looked upon his *personal opinions* as "straw" and gave vent to his joy in the faith through glorious hymns that celebrated, in the fullest sense of the word, the Mystery of Faith, the Real Presence of Jesus in the Sacrament.

It was once said that the first curse of the Almighty on those who deny Him is to deprive them of their sense of humor, to leave them without joy. I submit, that the first convincing proof that faith has triumphed over theological polemic and that we are renewed believers in the Risen Christ and in the God Who gives joy to our youth, will be when laughter is heard again and life and love are proclaimed with joy in our churches, our homes, our schools and our assemblies.

Last spring I visited the Chicanos, the Mexican-Americans of Texas. Shortly before I had been at a liturgy elsewhere where all the hymns were ecumenical, neutral, unrelated to any particular faith, however broad or bland, and more than enough to make me think it just possible that God is dead. But as I entered the church of the Chicanos, whose faith stands in no need of theological degrees from ecumenical centers of study, the whole church seemed on fire with the glad song of children singing, "To Be Alive, Oh God, What Joy To Be Alive!". They were laughing, exuberant, joyful. For a moment, I thought I had died and gone to heaven.

In the neo-clericalism now shaping up, we have a kind of para-hierarchy, a double *Magisterium,* made up of the successors of the Apostles, on the one hand, and the "professional theologians" on the other.

Recently, an Irish priest, who was a rebel from the day of his ordination, commented with a certain irony: Today we have two

67

hierarchies, that of the *Magisterium* and that of the "professional theologians." I always said that the one we had was more than enough for me!

Now, if the legitimate Hierarchy wants truly to clarify the situation and spread the Kingdom of God, it must preach the Word again, loudly and clearly, and let the "professional theologians" argue as they tend to do, far from the realities of things. The authentic Hierarchy, in its turn, as Chrysostom, Augustine, Paul, Peter, Athanasius, as the courageous Apostles who left Rome for England, for France, for the Slavic countries, for Germany, in a word, for the ends of the earth, will preach anew, with fresh joy the everlasting faith in God, in Jesus Christ, in the Church, where God in Christ Himself lives; in the life of the world to come, in love and hope; it must preach the joy that only the Cross makes possible.

We can say, therefore, that the people gathered here are not simply administrators, or people in whom that tendency predominates; nor are the theologians gathered here only "professionals," whether full-time or part-time. On the contrary, Men of God are gathered here, preachers, of the authentic divine Word. In other words, there are gathered here clergy, parents, religious and laity, who, savoring and loving their faith, deeply enjoying it, devote themselves to the catechetical mission, following in all things the example of Jesus Christ and the faith which He handed down to our fathers.

V

Christ Head of the Church and the Priest

At every turn in the Christian life we find ourselves face to face with Christ. Every reaction, every action, of every Christian, finds its main spring, its initial impulse, in Christ, Head of the Body which is the Church. Under all other questions of the Christian faith lies the question: "What think you of Christ? Whose Son is He?" At the core of all things which Christians hold sacred, all their cult as well as creed, is Christ. The Church is ultimately without meaning except as the living Body of Christ at work in the world. The Christian has no being, as a Christian, unless he can say "I live—no longer I alone, but Christ lives in me!" If the Christian is called to service in some special, even unique sense; if the Church is a "Servant Church," this is true only because the Christian, as the Church, is one with the "Servant Christ." The joys of the Christian, the sorrows of the Christian, like those of the Church in her varied moods of penance, refreshment, even spiritual triumphalism, all derive from Christ, depend on Christ. Christ is not merely a model or prototype; He is the living Head of every Christian, as of the Church.

How then, can we talk of the priest—the herald of the faith, the minister of Christian worship and sacramental life, the man of the Church, the "Alter Christus," who brings the life of the Word to the world and the life of God to men—how can we even think of the priest except in terms of Christ?

The mind of the Church on the priest is thus summed up in Vatican II, which is properly seen more as a point of arrival for

69

the collective mind of the Church certainly in the present stage of the authentic growth of the Church, rather than a point of departure for disparate and conflicting concepts of priesthood or anything else Catholic: "Priests, although they do not possess the highest degree of priesthood, and although they are dependent on the bishops in the exercise of their power, are nevertheless united with the bishops in sacerdotal dignity. By the power of the sacrament of orders, in the image of Christ the eternal high Priest, they are consecrated to preach the Gospel and shepherd the faithful and to celebrate divine worship, so that they are true priests of the New Testament. Partakers of the function of Christ the sole mediator, on their level of ministry, they announce the divine word to all. They exercise their sacred function especially in the eucharistic worship or the celebration of the Mass by which, acting in the person of Christ and proclaiming his mystery, they unite the prayers of the faithful with the sacrifice of their Head and until the coming of the Lord they represent and apply the only sacrifice of the New Testament, namely, that of Christ offering himself once for all a spotless victim to the Father. For the sick and sinners among the faithful, they exercise the ministry of alleviation and reconciliation and they present the needs and the prayers of the faithful to God the Father. Exercising within the limits of their authority the function of Christ as shepherd and head, they gather together God's family as a brotherhod all of one mind, and lead them in the Spirit, through Christ, to God the Father. In the midst of the flock they adore him in spirit and in truth. Finally, they labor in word and doctrine, believing what they have read and pondered in the law of God, teaching what they have believed, and putting in practice what they have taught" (*Constitution on the Church*, par. 28).

It would be difficult to imagine renunciation of self and identity with Christ, in work, in thought, in desire, in personality itself, more complete than that here described. The doing of Christ's work on every level and to the utter replacement of their own; the absorption of their time and their objectives in His, the immolation in and with Him of their very selves; the functioning "in His person" and not their own—all this in thought, word and deed is the ideal and the goal of the priest.

Truly the priest sacrifices all individuality, every thing that sets him apart, in his oneness with Christ; in Gertrud von le Fort's unforgettable line: "The priest at the altar has no face!" Nothing individualizes him—or nothing *should*. Priests acquire their relationship to Christ, in all the derived powers yet total dependence which that relationship carries with it, from and through their relationship to their Bishops. This, too, is clearly set forth in the Vatican Council Constitution on the Church:

"Christ, whom the Father has sanctified and sent into the world, has through his Apostles, made their successors, the bishops, partakers of his consecration and his mission. They have legitimately handed on to different individuals in the Church various degrees of participation in this ministry. Thus the divinely established ecclesiastical ministry is exercised on different levels by those who from antiquity have been called bishops, priests and deacons . . . ".

"Priests, prudent cooperators with the episcopal order, its aid and instrument, called to serve the people of God, constitute one priesthood with their bishop although bound by a diversity of duties. Associated with their bishop in a spirit of trust and generosity, they make him present in a certain sense in the individual local congregations and take upon themselves, as far as they are able, his duties and the burden of his care, and daily discharge them with zeal. As they sanctify and govern, under the bishop's authority, that part of the Lord's flock entrusted to them, they make the universal Church visible in their own locality and bring an efficacious assistance to the building up of the whole body of Christ. Intent always upon the welfare of God's children, they must strive to lend their effort to the pastoral work of the whole diocese, and even of the entire Church. On account of this sharing in their priesthood and mission, let priests sincerely look upon the bishop as their father and reverently obey him. And let the bishop regard his priests as his co-workers and as sons and friends, just as Christ called His disciples no longer servants but friends. All priests, both diocesan and religious, by reason of orders and ministry, fit into this body of bishops and priests, and serve the good of the whole Church according to their vocation and the grace given to them."

But does not this special corporate relationship to Christ, to the bishop and to one another, constitute priests a species of "class," even worse a "caste" apart, not to say an "undemocratic" structure, all of this uncongenial to our contemporary modes of thought? Are not the emotional overtones of these phrases not merely offensive to modern ears, but almost horrendous to a culture which, characterized though it be with built-in divisions, and even gross inequalities, has long since hypnotized itself by seductive phrases of "liberty, fraternity and equality" without reference to Christ, indeed in rejection of Christ, and has suddenly sought, quite apart from Christ or at most by analogies to His teachings, an application of these concepts in a secular sense.

The plain fact is, however, that the priesthood, as the episcopate, in any Catholic sense, though one in Christ and united through Him to one another by ties which have no part of the vocabulary or values of an order without Christ, save by equivocal analogies, are separate functions, separate callings, separate service, though all in the same Christ, and in behalf of the same people of God.

Let it be acknowledged, then, without shame, confusion or equivocation, that, even as all Christians "are not of this world, as I am not of the world" (in Christ's phrases descriptive of Himself) so His bishops, to whom in special manner He spoke His words of *distinction* but not *separation* from the world, and His priests are "in the world, but not of it." Analogies to the structures of the world are always to be weighed with great care when there is talk of the nature of the episcopal office and its relation to the world, as distinct from Christ. So, too, quite beyond their general priesthood and Christian fraternity, their "holy citizenship" and vocation to service among and within the entire servant Church (or praying Church or teaching Church, or suffering Church, or militant Church, or triumphant Church, or eschatological Church) priests have an ordination apart yet within that unity, and a brotherhood (be it called by whatever analogous figure of speech may suit the culture or spirit of a given moment in history); they have a "place apart" within the Church, so long as they are in communion with their bishops, and that place is all their own. This is the common, constant testimony of the Catholic Faith; it is the explicit teaching of Vatican Council II:

"In virtue of their common sacred ordination and mission, all priests are bound together in intimate brotherhood, which naturally and freely manifests itself in mutual aid, spiritual, as well as material, pastoral as well as personal, in their meetings and in communion of life, of labor and charity.

"Let them, as fathers in Christ, take care of the faithful whom they have begotten by baptism and their teaching. Becoming from the heart a pattern of the flock, let them so lead and serve their *local community* that it may worthily be called by that name, the Church of God. Let them remember that by their daily life and zeal they must present an image of a truly sacerdotal and pastoral ministry to the faithful and the unbelievers, to Catholics and non-Catholics, and that to all they bear witness to the truth and life, and as good shepherds seek those also, who though baptized in the Catholic Church have fallen away from the use of the sacraments, or even from the faith."

We have underscored the phrase *local Church* because in the *local Church,* provided it be in communion with Rome, the entire Church is realized, and priests, laity and apostolic works alike, (always together with the bishop: *nihil sine episcopo*) find their place in that total body of Christ which is the Church.

Such work, such testimony, such special participation in the ministry and mandate of Jesus Christ on the part of priest particularly, is essentially and peculiarly sacerdotal and in a special sense, "separate but not distinct" from the world. This does not mean that the distinctions between the "priestly people" and the "ordained priestly ministers" is such as to leave either, specifically the priests, without reference to the temporal order (the order, in a sense, "of the world"), but it does mean that their respective holy witnesses and works of the general priestly Church may and should have a Christ-like difference, Pope John's curious remark, addressed pointedly to priests, that Jesus Christ, given His priesthood, neither indulged in sport nor in politics, must be exaggerated to exclude chaplains to football teams or even to Civil Senates; it does not exclude the extraordinary ministry of the priestly coach in sport or even the exceptional priestly prime minister. It is far from meaning that the layman may not be called precisely to exercise the general priesthood which came with his baptism in these and other vocations, some of them more, some of them less conventional, but all of them channels through which the priestly Church sanctifies, consecrates and renews the world. But Pope John did mean (as Don Luigi Sturzo notably recognized in our day) that the ordained priesthood is bound by laws of its own and is a *status,* an order, and work apart.

Indeed the Council issues a clear call to the service of the temporal order in the special service expected of the priest, not merely as consistent with the rest of the priestly calling, but in accordance with that priesthood of all the sacerdotal Church, the ministry of reconciliation essential to Christ a general imperative for all the baptized, but a primary office of the Bishop and his ordained priests.

The Council's teaching in this connection is manifold and scattered, but so far as ordained priests are concerned and their special responsibilities towards work for peace as an aspect of the *ministry of reconciliation,* that teaching is all brought together in the *Constitution on the Church* at the end of paragraph 28 in terms of the chief need which the temporal order has of the Church's witness and service:

"Because the human race today is becoming more and more a civic, economic and social unity, it is the more necessary that priests, by combining their resources under the leadership of the bishops and the Supreme Pontiff, should eliminate everything that separates, so that the whole human race may be brought into the unity of the family of God."

Christ is Chief of all things, but above all of the priestly order. He is the Head of the Church not only in an organizational sense, but in the organic sense so emphasized by St. Paul in his doctrine of the Mystical Body, but by Christ Himself in His similitudes of the vine and the branches, the living unity which makes His people, above all His Apostles and priests, incapable of salutary action save in dependence on His Will, His Life, His Headship. The Church has no action, nor power to act, except it originate in Christ, the Head of all the Body, the principle of all its life, the Chief of all its service. So, too, but even more, of the priest. *All of which means that if the Church in all its members must share the heart, mind, tongue and hand of Christ, being subject to Him as Head, the priest to the extent that he is priest, must accept an identity even more complete, must bear even more intimate a witness, not of his own ideas, not of any partisan group, or class, or clique . . . only of Christ. Otherwise he is himself, but he is not Christ at work in the world. Otherwise he may be a person in some philosophical sense, but he is not a priest in any theological sense.*

Father Karl Rahner, unfooled by the rhetoric of the hour, especially such rhetoric as invites priests to "prove" their Christian testimony by doing the works of the baptized layman in the secular order, sums this up for every Christian but in supreme degree for the priest when he writes: "Today the true non-conformism can consist in *fidelity* to a holy tradition deriving from the most ancient wisdom of the Gospel, namely that of swimming against the current, proclaiming the folly of the Cross." This is St. Paul's description of the special preaching work of the Apostle, the bishop and his priest.

Christ said of his priestly Church that in doing its work it must always be a "sign of contradiction" to the prevailing spirit of the world; how much more so must be the case of the ordained priest whose every word resounds the mind of Christ the Head, every act responds to a dictate of that Head, whose relationship to Christ, whenever it reveals itself, is entirely special, apart from that of all members of the "priestly people, the royal priesthood" by which St. Peter identified all those sealed with Baptism. That unique "distinct but not separate" presence of the ordained priest within the Church by which the priest enjoys or is burdened by special responsibilities to the Head which is Christ, the liturgy describes in the Votive Mass of Our Lord Jesus Christ, the Eternal High Priest, when it prays: "O God, by whom Your only-begotten Son has been established High and Eternal Priest, to the glory of Your majesty and for the salvation of mankind, grant that those He has chosen as ministers and dispensers of His mysteries may be found faithful in fulfilling the ministry they have accepted. Through Christ our Lord."

The Epistle of the same Mass justifies that prayer by giving its theological premises in the special ties between Christ-Head and each of His priests as these are spelled out in the Epistle to the Hebrews: (Hebrews 5, 1-11) "Every high priest taken from among men is ordained for men in the things that appertain to God; that he may offer up gifts, and sacrifices for sins; who can have compassion on them that are ignorant and that err: because he himself also is compassed with infirmity: and therefore he ought, as for the people so also for himself, to offer for sins. Neither doth any man take the honor to himself, but he that is called by God, as Aaron was. So Christ also did not glorify Himself that He might be made a high priest; but He that said unto Him: 'Thou art My Son, this day have I begotten Thee.' As he saith also in another place 'Thou art a priest for ever, according to the order of Melchisedech.' Who in the days of His flesh, with a strong cry and tears, offering up prayers and supplications to Him that was able to save Him from death, was heard for His reverence. And whereas indeed He was the Son of God, He learned obedience by the things which He suffered. And being consummated, He became, to all that obey Him, the cause of eternal salvation: called by God a high priest, according to the order of Melchisedech.''

This "theology of the priesthood" has behind it 2000 years of the preaching of Apostles sent by Christ Himself; of meditation on that preaching by the Fathers of the West and those of the East; of the speculation of theologians down to just before our own minute in history; of the tenacity of the *Magisterium* by which the truth in the Church is preserved; of the Laws by which that Truth is applied, *humano modo,* in every age and under changing conditions.

It is this "theology of the priesthood"—Christ the Head of every priest as well as of the Church—Christ the principal agent as well as source of all priestly power and authority, as opposed to any theory of the priest as the voice or delegate of the community, however Christian, however Christ-centered, — which warranted the witness of John Chrysostom in his second homily on 2 Timothy 4: "Christ gave the same thing to His disciples which the priests now minister. One is not less than the other, for it is not men who consecrate it, but Christ Himself who bestows sanctifications. For as the words which God spoke are the same which the priest now utters, so is the offering the same, just as the baptism which he gave. *Thus the whole is a matter of faith.*"

It is this same "theology" which enables the same Chrysostom to speak of the hand of the priest not as a hand empowered by a count of hands at a convention of Christians, let alone of a humanly informed, even sincere "secular city," *but as the hand of Christ:*

"For if they who had touched the hem of His garment drew so much power from Him; how much more they that possess Him entire? Now to draw near with faith is not only to receive the bread offered, but also to touch it with a pure heart and to be so moved as if one approached Christ Himself . . . Believe therefore, that that very supper is being celebrated at which He Himself reclined. For man does not make this, and Christ that, but both this and that are the work of Christ. When you see the priest offering the consecrated bread, do not think that the priest is doing this, for it is the hand of Christ which is extended. For just as when a priest baptizes, it is not he who baptizes, but God, Who touches your head with invisible power so that neither Angel nor Archangel nor anyone else dare draw near and touch you" (*Homily 50 on Matthew 2-3*).

So, too, it is Chrysostom who, uncontradicted by fifteen centuries of Catholic thought, says: "Christ is present, and he who set that table *then,* sets this one *now.* For it is not a man who brings it about that the offerings become the body and blood of Christ, but it is Christ Himself, Who was crucified for us. The priest stands fulfilling a *role,* when he speaks these words, but the power and grace are God's. This is my body, He says. This sentence changes the elements which lie before Him" (*Homily on Betrayal of Judas*).

In a word, as Bastian observes: "Just as an instrument is incapable of accomplishing a task unless the principal cause guide it, so the work of the priest receives its salvific power from the grace of God." Thus is proclaimed the dependence of the priest on Christ-Head, through the appointed "structures" of the Church.

All this is confirmed, in terms which almost seem to have been chosen for certain theories presently bruited about, by an important document of early canon law, originating in Egypt at the beginning of the fourth century.

Describing how Christ is at all times the Chief Priest, the Head, the Egyptian document recites: "As the first presbyter, the only true chief priest is our Lord Jesus Christ, Who did not grasp for Himself the honor, but the Father ordained Him, and as He is the chief priest for us, *so He offered spiritual sacrifice to God the Father before He was crucified,* and He commanded us to do likewise. And there were others with us who believed in Him, but He does not grant to all who believe in Him to be priests, nor to obtain the order of ordination to the priesthood like us. And after His ascension we offered, according to the ordinance, the holy bloodless oblation." (*Apostolic Church Order* 72). What, one asks with baffled mind and bated breath, would the believing authors of this piece of Faith and Order have thought of the sentimental but stupid invitation of the ordained priest who invites the congregation to pronounce with him the words of consecration in "our" sacrifice?

Again, in brief, the ordained priest is the minister of Christ, not of the Community, and it was Christ, Who is sole priest, Who commanded His followers to offer His sacrifice. This is done in accordance with the laws governing liturgical worship, which have been handed down from the beginning.

St. Leo the Great loved to recall and rejoice in how Christ works in His priest. He did so in pastoral, but strictly theological terms: "Consequently, dearly beloved, it is not with bold presumption that we, mindful of the divine goodness, honor the day on which we accepted the office of the priesthood. For we confess in all gratitude and truth that, whatever good we may do in the exercise of our ministry, it is Christ Himself who works in us. Hence we rejoice not in ourselves, who can do nothing without Him, but in Him Who gives us the possibility of acting for Him" (*Sermon* 5, 4; *PL* 54, 154).

Or again: "the pardon of God cannot be obtained through the suppliant prayers of priests. For the 'mediator between God and man, the man Christ Jesus' (1 Timothy 2, 5) has given this power to the rulers of the Church, that they assign the performance of a penance to those who have confessed, and, after they have been cleansed by salutary satisfaction, admit them to communion through the door of reconcilation . . . He must not put off his conversion to God from day to day, and chose for it a time which is so restricted that there will scarcely be a sufficient interval for the confession of the penitent or reconcilation by the priest" (*Letter* 108, 2, 5).

The power of forgiveness is entrusted to the rulers of the Church, and this clearly by Christ, not the community. This forgiveness is obtained, as is clear from the concluding sentence of St. Leo where the role of the priest is underscored. It may well be that some contemporary "theologies" may open up refreshed lines of thought on the "communitarian" aspects of both sin and virtue, and on the "structures" of the exercise of authority, including the power of forgiveness, and the choice of those who aptly exercise it, but even on these points the burden of proof lies entirely on the originators of the new "theologies." Nothing can diminish the force and the unique dominion of Christ, the Head of every priest as of the Church, and still remain, in any minimal sense, authentic Catholic doctrine or Christian tradition. Not even an angel from Heaven, let alone a theologian filled with figures of speech from one or another form of democracy or other political theory, nor the most benign Protestant participant in a dialogue designed to help us share one another's theological insights or sacramental experiences, can preach any other doctrine without falling under St. Paul's oft quoted anathema!

It might be profitable to explore some of the practical issues of this concept of the Head-Ship of Christ over every priest (not only over the Christian community within which the priest of Christ acts as "liturgical president," as the current phrase has it, when we gather for Mass); if so the attentive reader will gain greatly from *The Post Conciliar Priest* by Father Raymond A. Tartre, S.S.S., which Bishop Ernest J. Primeau describes as a "must" in the library of every post conciliar priest who seeks security and consolation in his vocation, joy and happiness in his work.

Other literature pours constantly from the press.

It may well be necessary that we rediscover the way in which the priest, precisely because called and sent by God Himself, as Aaron was, is our ordinary contact with the "holy," the "sacred" even in an age of the "secular." If so, we must meditate why the "declericalization of the priest," an alleged demand of the Secular City and of the alleged whisperings of the Holy Spirit in our "democratic age," has placed in crisis the very concept of the *Sacred.* In that case, to recover our sense of the *Sacred* under everything secular, particularly in the priest, to appreciate once again, as did our fathers in the faith, the Head-Ship of Christ in everything that pertains to priest and Church alike, we will do well to study with attention what Father Battista Mondin has to say about the "singularity of the priest" in the established doctrine of the Church that has always understood what the recent Council (and St. Peter) underlines concerning "the universality of the priesthood" in a priestly Church. We should most carefully study what Father Mondin notes in his book, *La declericalizzazione del prete: Sacralità in crisi?* (Borla 1969), concerning a process, already under way, which seeks, above all, to involve, to his hurt, the priest at the center of its debates and experiments: "The three characteristic aspects of his personality (holy orders, special ministry and celibacy) are subjected to sensationalism, vivisection, criticism." Father Mondin points out some current scholars have found these indissolubly linked to a type of society already disappeared from the scene, a society they denominate as "sacral." Hence they call for a radical and systematic "declericalization," or reappraisal of priesthood.

This, in turn, calls for three logical stages: 1) elimination of the "clerical structure" of the Church (with the suppression of holy orders); 2) reduction of the power and the authority of the clergy (to expand that of the laity[1];) 3) "lightening" the ascetical burdens of priestly life (eliminating clerical celibacy). Father Mondin promises submits these "stages" to serene and objective study.

It may be time for a complete restudy of the Catholic concept of the priesthood especially against the background of certain contrived theories of the origins of its nature, functions and obligations, origins attributed to imperial, feudal or "sacral" civilizations (when, by the way, in these last 2000 years was there a "sacral" civilization?) and against the pretensions of a "purer" concept of the priesthood, more suited to the "purer" people of an age of "democracy." If so, there are still the scriptures to ponder, the Fathers of the Church to study, the great theologians to review, a multipilicty of recent and not so recent "standard" works on the priesthood to re-read. There are at least three major encyclicals by Popes in this century analyzing the Catholic priesthod and the special relationship it gave the Popes in question to Christ, their Head, entirely apart from their papacy and consequent "vicarship" for Christ. But fortunately Father Clement Dillenschneider, C.SS.R., has given us in several languages two volumes which tell the whole story of Christ, the One Priest of the New Law; the clear mission from Christ, distinct from the general priesthood of all

---

1 It is, of course, assumed that Father Mondin recognizes, with all, the 'royal priesthood' proper to the laity, the historic role of the laity, male and female, in the life, thought and action of the church and looks forward to the due development of the role of the laity in the life of the church. I say this as the bishop who, by historical accident, raised the question of the theology of the laity in Vatican Council II and served as chairman of the commission preparing the Council's statement of the merest premises of that theology, premises in no way challenging or negating the totally different nature of the ordained ministerial priesthood. I say it also as one who preaches the theology of the laity in general and the historic contribution of specific laymen to the essential work of the church. Inside and outside the Council I have been kept conscious by believing laymen of the distinction between my priesthood and theirs, a distinction which made us in no way separate as Christians or, indeed, as brethren of Christ, who possessed a distinct priesthood and powers proper to himself.

members of the Church that comes with Baptism, and of those priests of Christ the Chief Priest, those who act *in persona Christi* as *ministerial* agents of Christ, from the Pope at the head of the hierarchy, established by Christ, to the most recent priest *ordained to holy orders* and serving the rest of the baptized (and, please God, the unbaptized) in the most obscure corner of God's earth. Volume I of Father Dillenschneider's book is called in its English version, "Christ the One Priest and We His Priests." It tells, I repeat, the whole story, recalls the ancient truth and anticipates the rhetoric shaping up unto the ruin of the priesthood, the Church, the very sense of the divine (the "sacred") as distinct from and essential to the valid secular, natural and even profane elements of human civilization, ancient, medieval and modern.

Herder and Herder, publishing the English edition, does not go too far in saying, as they do, that this book, because of its scholarship, its clarity, its setting down of practical concepts and directives, "will help make of the priest who reads It what the world of the present day expects of him—*that he be a priest*," above all, a priest given to meditation.

The notion of meditation brings us to the work of Father René Voillaume, whose retreats in the Vatican have so helped in priestly renewal. The latest of his Vatican retreats is entitled: *Con Gesù nel Deserto* (Morcelliana), in its French edition put out by Fayard. It treats of our relations with Jesus-Our Head with great simplicity and sublime inspiration.

Every Christian vocation is covered by Father Voillaume, but two chapters reflect with special care and acumen on *Priests and Pastors with Jesus in His Church*. They are not to be missed.

But perhaps the answer lies not merely in casual reading or the recollection of hallowed wisdom and scholarship. It lies, one cannot doubt, in a whole new effort at priestly *formation* that is inspired by the prayer that Christ may remain the Head of every priest and every priest may become, ever more clearly, the living, active, holy agent of Christ and therefore His Church, involved in their priestly functions proclaimed by Guitton: "I fear that the priests of the future, in their noble aspiration to mix with us, may be tempted to draw too close to us, wasting time and energy trying to speak our peculiar jargon, to adopt our ways and attitudes, our flurried lives and worldly occupations. Listening to my young priest-friends I feel uncomfortably conscious that they do not seem to appreciate sufficiently the dignity of their vocation. The priest is not a welfare officer.

"I say to them: 'What we laymen ask of you is to give us God, by means of your exclusive powers of absolution and consecration; that you remain constantly mindful that we look up to you as representatives amongst us of the Eternal, as ambassadors of the Absolute. Starved for the Absolute, we laymen need to have you in our midst as persons who will prove to us that He can exist, and is, in fact, closer to us than we can imagine.' "

VI
Priestly Maturity

The recent Instruction *"Ratio fundamentalis institutionis sacerdotalis,"*[1] published by the Sacred Congregation for Catholic Education, indicates as the purpose of seminary formation the attainment of *sacerdotal maturity,* which maturity presupposes, as essential and integral to it, the presence of certain human elements which guarantee a greater efficacy, fruitfulness and stability of the priestly ministry in the Church.

It appears opportune, therefore, to focus our attention, as we intend to do in this paper, on one single affirmation of the Instruction. "The building of a total priest is by its very nature such that *throughout his life,* but especially in the first years after his sacred ordination, *his formation should be continued and perfected ever more completely"* (Ratio fundamentalis institutionis sacerdotalis, n. 100).[2]

This argues that the mature priest must also be a mature man and it suggests, by inevitable implications, that whenever a defective priest, a man unstable in his priesthood, appears in the Christian community, underneath the unfulfilled priest there may well be an immature man. Priestly defections, priestly unhappiness, priestly crises of whatever kind may have various explanations, as they do in the lives of other men; but the most common one that shows up in the priest who loses or compromises his commitment to the priesthood, especially in the area of alcoholism, uncontrolled sexuality and such complications of priestly efficiency as hypochondria, is not so much lack of idealism as a priest—this remains

---

1 S. Gongregatio pro Institutione Catholica, **Ratio fundamentalis institutionis sacerdotalis, Romae** 1970, p. 66.
2 **Ibid.,** n. 100.

as a further torment in such cases—but personal and priestly immaturity.

It is our present purpose then to present the figure of priesthood in terms of priestly maturity, both human and supernatural, and to argue that the realization of maturity constitutes the principal objective of seminary formation.

The purpose of seminary formation for the priesthood and of the continuation of that formation after the seminary, particularly for young priests but also for all us priests, is the formation of a *mature man, a responsible man, a priest who is therefore fulfilled and faithful.*

All men are called by God to that self-realization that we call maturity and that constitutes perfection; Christians, but above all *priests* are the objects of a special call in this regard. Early in the Old Testament Yahweh charged His People to be mature, perfect and holy: "You shall be holy unto me, because I the Lord am holy, and I have separated you from other people, that you should be mine" (Leviticus 20, 26). Likewise the Lord Jesus in His first public sermon on the mountain of the Beatitudes renewed this call: "You therefore are to be perfect, even as your heavenly Father is perfect" (Matthew 5, 48). As a consequence all Christians, and, one repeats, above all the apostles and their successors, together with their priestly collaborators are called to be perfect. Their vocation is not to a perfection like to that of the angels, but like to God Himself, like to the heavenly Father, like to His Beloved Son, their Eternal and High Priest, the likeness constituting in the fact that they seek and, by God's grace, attain the total fulfillment of the being that is theirs as God possesses the total perfection of the Being that is His.

This maturity and perfection of a man is also the theme of the apostolic exhortations of St. Paul: "But to each one of us grace was given according to the measure of Christ's bestowal. Thus it says, 'Ascending on high, he led away captives; he gave gifts to men.' Now this, 'he ascended,' what does it mean but that he also first descended into the lower parts of the earth? He who descended, he it is who ascended also above all the heavens, that he might fill all things. And he himself gave some men as apostles, and some as prophets, others again as evangelists, and others as pastors and teachers, in order to perfect the saints for a work of ministry, for building up the body of Christ, until we all attain to the unity of the faith and of the deep knowledge of the Son of God, *to perfect manhood, to the mature measure of the fullness of Christ."* Hence the end of seminary and post-seminary formation is the formation of a mature man who will thus become the basis of a complete priest "in the mature measure of the full of Christ" Himself, for the priest is truly *another Christ;* he is the minister and "servant of Christ" and of the Church, as he is the guardian and dispenser of the mysteries of God (1 Corinthians 4, 1-4).

Certain aspects of contemporary culture and civilization, more particularly perhaps within the family community itself, but certainly in the general community, do not make easy a ready response to a priestly vocation and its equally easy realization. Even less do these circumstances of our times lend aid to that coming to maturity, even as a man, which priestly perfection presupposes. The situation in which the contemporary priestly personality finds himself as a man must therefore be described as *negative* in terms of his prospects for priestly maturity if only because it so greatly increases the personal responsibility of the young candidate for the priesthood for his own formation. Responsibility for bringing to attainment his own personal progress, for drawing out of himself (we must never forget that the root meaning of education comes from *educere*) his own personal potential and thus achieving maturity falls back almost entirely upon himself, the priestly aspirant, in an age of technology and a culture chiefly concerned with the world outside the person rather than within. Seminarians and young priests of another generation had an advantage that came with the very education constitutive of the liberal arts tradition, a tradition involving a humanism which was more concerned with

87

the person than with the machinery of his life and which summed up and transmitted the wisdom and the discipline of the ages as a counteractive to the preoccupations of a bewildering knowledge explosion, especially with regard to things, and a technology pre-occupied with externals, however convenient and however useful.

This humanism, particularly when it became influenced and elevated by Christianity, transmitted to the seminarian and the priest not merely the knowledge but, what is much more important, the wisdom accumulated in the Western World by the learning of Greek civilization, the discipline of the Roman heritage, and the mystical insights of the Judaeo-Christian tradition. I hasten to note that the philosophical, literary and religious traditions of the Eastern World had like normative elements, but in the Western World most assuredly the liberal arts tradition plus religious faith provided a heritage which may be summed up, somewhat over-simply perhaps but with real point, in three norms for which we were indebted to the Greek, Roman and Judaeo-Christian tradi-tions, almost in successive stages which added up to the Christian culture and, in no small measure to the culture of the Western World.

Each of those norms could be expressed in two words. The Greeks, intellectual and philosophical, left to us the formula: *Know thyself*. In this formula the philosopher who transmitted to us the two major streams of Greek philosophy summed up the contribu-tion of that world to our maturity as men and, in the case of those who pursued an ecclesiastical vocation, as priests. All knowledge begins with knowledge of one's self and whatever other knowledge we may possess, however vast, however erudite, may easily prove a force of personal disintegration unless he who possesses the knowl-edge first of all *knows himself*: his capacities, his limitations, his virtues and those inclinations toward evil which the traditional spirituality called his "dominant passion." It is as true in our own day as it was in the day of Socrates: All knowldege begins with self-knowledge.

In no one is this more true than it is in the candidate for the priesthood. From the first days of his formation he must necessarily know more about himself than any outsider, however keen his discernment of spirits, can possibly know. Indeed, only to the extent that he knows himself can he provide the essential elements of the knowledge which those who advise him, guide him, help form him can possess. He must know himself in depth, perceiving clearly his own motivation and weighing carefully his own potentialities toward the realization of that motivation. He must have gazed within himself and reflected upon himself sincerely and realistically in order to evaluate his physical condition, his psychological aptitudes, his moral potential, his religious, emotional and intellectual capacities. Only on the basis of his self-knowledge can he answer for himself or provide others with the elements of the answer as to how prepared he is to respond to a seeming call to the priesthood with a decision that is carefully weighed, responsible and, to return to our key word, mature.

If he thinks himself to hear the voice of the Lord saying, "follow Me," "Come, follow me, and I will make you fishers of men" (Matthew 4, 19), he can respond with at least the beginnings of maturity, "Behold, I come . . . to do thy will, O God" (Hebrews 10, 7), which means on the basis of a self-knowledge which has traditionally been part of a demand of our culture and the heritage available to us.

A knowledge of what constitutes a divine vocation—the vocation of Christ Himself to the priesthood—is, of course, indispensable. But the response to such a vocation, presupposes a human self-knowledge which, realistically, humbly and objectively, brings under one's own study and one's own eventual control the forces within one's self which make for maturity. The blend of these two forms of knowledge, knowledge of Christ and knowledge of one's self, yields the indispensable conditions of human maturity both in the seminarian and in the priest. The former will provide the characteristic difference in the man who becomes a priest,

89

another Christ; but the latter must be prior in time if the blend of the two is to be effective.

If the Greeks were intellectuals and thus contributed to our heritage the intellectual formula *"know thyself,"* the Roman world was more nearly what we would probably call *voluntarist.* Its culture was largely derived and its characteristic contribution to the liberal arts tradition and the civilization of the Western World was typified by its *planning,* its purposefulness, its road building, its genius for law and for empire. We can, again with a certain but not excessive simplicity, summarize its contribution in the two words, *"rule thyself."* Added to the Greek *"know thyself,"* this norm provided the basis of a humanism which was at the heart of the culture of the Mediterranean World and which was later to give wise and disciplined Christians of every kind, but especially priests, the advantage of self-knowledge and self-discipline.

Jesus was to say quite simply: *"deny thyself"* by which He made the admonition to rule thyself and the perfection that is self-discipline even more effective and programmatic. In the Gospel of St. Matthew we read the following words of the Lord: "If anyone wishes to come after me, let him deny himself, and take up his cross, and follow me. For he who would save his life will lose it; but he who loses his life for my sake will find it" (Matthew 16, 24-25).

These words of the Master became the foundation of priestly self-discipline for generations; they gave a greater nobility to what might otherwise have been the mere stoicism of the Roman quality at its best. The doctrine of Jesus concerning obedience and the manner in which He linked obedience to His commands to love for His Person ("You are my friends if you do those things that I have commanded," and the like, cf. John 14, 1-16 generally), is His form of the Roman insistence on the formation of the will and of the centrality of law. Whenever Jesus spoke of Love He did so in terms of Law, a new commandment, an act of the will, involving the entire self, to be sure, but depending on the measure in which we have blended self-discipline with self-knowledge.

The observance of the commandments of the Lord and of the discipline of the Church early became, on the basis of the words of Jesus Himself, the guarantee of the authenticity of any Christian's love for Christ and for the Church; *a fortiori,* it became the essence of the priesthood and the evidence of the maturity of a priest.

The contemporary man who becomes a priest may have little patience with this contribution of the Roman heritage or the requirements which Christ, personally or through His Church, includes under His Law of Love. Our generation increasingly seeks wider and more diverting highways, broad highways with new frontiers made possible more by machinery than by personal requirements or considered motivation. But for the Christian, and again most especially for the seminarian and the priest, such *autostrade* or many-laned turnpikes are part of the conveniences of this world, to be used when needed but not serving as a norm for the spiritual life. For these the words of the Lord, demanding self-discipline, remain as pertinent as they were before the age of superhighways: "Enter by the narrow gate. For wide is the gate and broad is the way that leads to destruction, and many there are who enter that way. How narrow the gate and close the way that leads to life! And few there are who find it" (Matthew 7, 13-14).

These are the words in which Christ still addresses His seminarians and His priests. There is nothing stoic about them, as their contemporary critics pretend, for they are charged with love and call out to love, a love which expresses itself, thanks to self-discipline, with free and loving obedience to the Will of the Father. Such obedience, even unto the death of the cross, was a divine form of the human instinct to *rule thyself* and self-discipline which the Romans transmitted to us. It constituted the very essence of the priesthood of Christ and His title to glory: "He humbled himself . . . becoming obedient even unto death, even the death of the cross" (Philippians 2, 6-8). This obedience was obedience to a mandate, a law imposed upon Him by His Father, but it was a free obedience made possible by that self-discipline which was pre-eminent in Christ and indispensable in the priest.

If it be true, as I take it to be, that the Greek and Roman heritage, on the natural level of our western liberal arts tradition, with their respective contributions of *know thyself* and *rule thyself,* contribute mightily not merely to the climate but the content of growth unto maturity in the candidates to the prieshood in he pre-technological, pre-phenomenological period in our cultural history, it is not less true that the Hebrew prophetic tradition and certainly the Christian revelation integrated these and lifted them to the level where maturity in Christ became possible. The Judaeo-Christian tradition added its two-word formula of *give thyself.*

It did so in terms of the spirit of self-giving in the form of the acceptance of divine election by the Jews, the voluntary segregation and commitment of a people for the sake of an ideal which constituted the Jews a nation. It did so by the symbolic gift of himself in total obedience and unquestioning generosity by the symbolic action of Abraham, prepared to give himself in his son at the request of God. The rule of life summed up in *give thyself* was, of course, perfectly demonstrated and exemplified for all time by the emptying of Himself, the unwavering commitment and the gift of Himself on the cross of the Incarnate Son of God.

In terms of the vocation to the priesthood, self-knowledge and self-discipline made possible a self-giving in response to one's vocation that was at once, *total, free, definitive* and, which is the point of our present considerations, *fully mature.* It involved commitment to Christ, the Eternal High Priest, to His Church, and to the service of God's people as basically structured and planned by Him, and to the portion of the flock committed to one's unselfish care.

To this total and conscious self-giving to Christ and to the unqualified manner in which one made himself available to the service of the Church, a young man was prepared during all the time of his stay in the seminary not merely by spiritual guidance and by the grace that came from the sacramental life of a seminarian, nor merely from his philosophical-theological cultural formation, but by the integration of all three of the formulae we have been discussing: self-knowledge, self-discipline, self-giving. It was a personal preparation, at once humane (humanistic) and Christian. It made it possible for grace to build on nature and it reduced the terrible danger of a conflict between nature and grace, between faith and reason, between the committed priest and the cultivated man such as has been the menace not only to priestly perseverance but to personal integrity since the distinctions of Descartes split the level of human preparation and of reason from that of priestly preparation and faith.

Self-giving must always be a *definitive* offering of one's self; it was traditionally symbolized in many ways, from the clipping of one's hair at tonsure to the symbolic step in sub-diaconate and the prostration of one's self in the sanctuary on the day of priestly ordination. New cultural forms will require and suggest new symbols and it appears almost certain that some, at least, of the traditional symbols may disappear entirely. But the heart of the matter remains perennial and constant. There is no self-knowledge which hides from one's self any area of his being; there is no self-discipline which exempts one from any area of his instinctual, physical or spiritual ilfe; there is no self-giving that is done with fingers crossed, mental reservations, divided heart, or looking back over one's shoulder. Jesus, using the last figure of speech, made that perfectly clear from the beginning of the Christian order; the Church, in her official teaching, at least, has never contradicted Him or been unfaithful to His mandate that priestly self-giving be integral, namely an offering of one's entire person, with all his gifts, charismatic and other, as these were received from God and as God asked them back in the form of service to others in the moment that He gave the Christian man his special vocation to the ministerial priesthood. Self-giving requires the gift of all one's soul

93

and all one's body: one's hands for the offering of the sacrifice of
Christ and the administration of the sacraments, one's mouth for
the proclaiming of the Word of God, one's heart and all its affec-
tions for the unqualified and undivided love of the things of God,
beginning with the humanity of His Son and extending, without
exception based on personal considerations, to all God's people,
most particularly those, as one's parish or school or other group,
to whom one is assigned not so much as the result of self-
preference or expression, but as part of one's self-giving.

A further motive which renders indispensable the offering of
one's very body is the necessity that mature priests play a special
part in that *completion* of Christ by the building up of His Mystical
Body which is the Church, in accordance with the plea of St. Paul:
"I rejoice now in the sufferings I bear for your sake; and what is
lacking of the sufferings of Christ *I fill up in my flesh* for his body,
which is the Church" (Colossians 1, 24). For all this Paul described himself as having been "crucified" once and for all with
Christ. He could express his own self-giving in terms of an identi-
fication with Christ so intimate as to make it possible for him to
say that he lived no longer as one apart or on his own but in such
fashion that "Christ lives in me." By this he meant no merely mystical presence of Christ in his spirit, in his obedient will or his
devoted mind; he meant that Christ lived in his very flesh and did
so because he himself, knowing that flesh in all its potential for
good or evil and dominating it in all the same potentials, responded
by total self-giving to that gift of Himself by Christ which had
made possible his life as a Christian and a priest. In his Epistle to
the Romans Paul addresses himself to all Christians, but in an
especial fashion, one cannot doubt, to the priests who must be the
models to Christians: "I exhort you therefore, brethren, by the
mercy of God, *to present your bodies as a sacrifice,* living, holy,
pleasing to God—your spiritual service" (Romans 12, 1).

Somehow our new culture, our changing civilization, our new
historical patterns of life and thought must make possible that

self-knowledge, self-discipline and self-giving which were once produced through the happy combination of the liberal arts culture, a theology based on the Gospels and a faith constant in the Christian community. For it is only with the realization of these three essential elements of maturity—self-knowledge, self-discipline and self-giving—that it becomes possible to talk of the *authenticity* of the ministerial priesthood as Catholicism has understood it from the beginning. It is only when these three elements have been verified in modern terms that we can speak of the priestly *identity,* the reality and efficacy of which in the contemporary world is so earnestly sought.[3]

Pope Pius XI, in his still valid encyclical on the priesthood, *Ad Catholici Sacerdotii,* summing up all the tradition of the Church from the beginning, felt prepared to draw a conclusion which may have to become the premise of the planning of contemporary bishops until the three formulae we have been dwelling upon are once again realized. Pope Pius said that if we cannot secure a sufficient number of the type of priests we have been describing, *then it is better to have only a few good priests in the service of the Church than to have many priests who are less than good inflicted on the faithful.*[4] Better a few priests and these mature, than hosts of priests and these immature, knowing neither themselves nor God, unprepared to rule themselves and therefore unfit to rule others, qualified in their self-giving and therefore inefficacious in their labors, personal or official.

We have touched upon certain essential elements of seminary life and of the formation of young priests in the light of Sacred Scripture and the humanistic tradition.

---

3 Confer the discourse of Pope Paul VI, **Sacerdoti autentici di Cristo e della Chiesa,** in "Insegnameti," VI, pp. 1052-1053; Paolo VI, **Il Sacerdozio, Ancora,** Milano 1970, pp. 149-150; Michele Card. Pellegrino, **Cosa aspetta la Chiesa torinese dai preti di domani — Il Seminario minore,** collana "Maestri della fede," n. 28, Elle Di Ci, Torino-Leumann 1970, p. 11.

4 Cf. A.A.S., 28 (1936) 44.

Vatican Council II has this to say: "(Priests) By the power of the sacrament of orders, and in the image of Christ the eternal High Priest (Hebrews 5, 1-10; 7, 24; 9, 11-28), they are consecrated to preach the gospel, shepherd the faithful, and celebrate divine worship as true priests of the New Testament" (*Lumen gentium*, n. 28).[5] To realize these objectives of their sacred vocation, priests are called continually to cultivate and develop their "self-giving" and self-discipline, as well as their self-knowledge. The requirements of this call have been developed by recent documents of the Sacred Congregation for Catholic Education, by repeated discourses of the Holy Father as these are summarized in a single book[6] and, in a programmatic way by the recent directives published both by the Congregation for Education[7] and the Congregation for the Clergy.[8]

The Council speaks clearly of the need for priestly maturity and perfection in the decree *Optatam totius,* especially when it calls upon Episcopal Conferences in the various parts of the world to provide for the *gradual* introduction of their young clergy into priestly life and action[9] with a constant provision for the renewal and increase of the spiritual, intellectual and pastoral resources of the clergy.[10] The documents published by not a few Episcopal Conferences give hope, sometimes strong, sometimes wistful, that new directions of life, thought and action are being linked to the ancient, perennial requirement of *priestly maturity*.

Intellectual maturity, above all in the sacred sciences, is solidly

---

5 Cost. **Lumen gentium**, n. 28.

6 Paolo VI, **Il Sacerdozio**, Ancora, Milano 1970, p. 344.

7 S. Congregatio pro Institutione Catholica, **Ratio fundamentalis**

8 S. Congregatio pro Clericis, **Litterae circulares ad Conferentiarum Episcopalium Praesides de permanenti cleri, maxime iunioris, institutione et formatione secundum placita Congregationis Plenariae die 18 Octobris habitae**, Typis Polyglottis Vaticanis (1969), p. 13. institutionis sacerdotalis, Roma 1970, p. 66.

9 Cf. n. 22.

10 Cf. **Litterae circulares ad Conferentiarum episcopalium Praesides**, n. 4; **Ratio fundamentalis**, nn. 100-101.

demanded by the ordained bishop of the candidate for the priesthood during the ordination ceremony. Priests, it is said, should be
mature in their learning. Their doctrine, evangelical and patristic
in its roots, should include a knowledge of the declarations of the
magisterium of the Church, above all of the Councils and of the
Chief Shepherds of Christendom, as well as a secure and balanced
grasp of theological principles, out of all of which they must blend
"a spiritual medicine for the People of God."[11]

Spiritual maturity expresses itself in a continued renewal of
that self-giving which we have seen to be the specifically Christian
contribution to the trinity of formulae we have suggested. It
becomes possible in the renunciation of one's self, one's life, one's
time, all that one is and does. Such self-giving is possible only with
Christ and in Christ and through Christ; it is liturgically expressed
in the Eucharistic celebration of the paschal mystery during Holy
Mass, but it does not end with the final words of the Mass. It is a
program of 365 days a year all the years of one's life.

Priests can seek perfection, indeed they are bound to seek it,
in obedience to the precept of the Lord: "You therefore are to be
perfect, even as your heavenly Father is perfect" (Matthew 5, 48).
This special obligation to seek perfection on the part of priests
derives from the fact that they, by means of their ordination which
is a further and distinct consecration to God beyond those made in
Baptism and Confirmation, are lifted to the level of living instruments of Christ, the Eternal High Priest, to continue in time His
literally divine work, which has caught up into itself all the effica-

---

11 Pont. Rom., **De Ordinatione Presbyterorum.** Cf. il decreto **Presbyterorum Ordinis,** n. 19; **Litterae circulares,** n. 5; **Ratio fundamentalis,**
nn. 100-101. Sometimes one thinks it would be far more conducive to
their maturity if priests spent more time in the reading and meditating
of Sacred Scriptures, the Fathers of the Church, the documents of the
magisterium, the works of the established theologians than in being
titillated by theological "novelties" (what Maritain called, with
slightly excessive impatience, "theological science fiction") and by a
sector of the Catholic press which has appointed itself conscience,
teacher and reformer of the Church.

cies of human nature to put these at the disposition of divine power and divine purposes. Thus consecrated with the anointing of the Holy Spirit and mandated by Christ, they mortify themselves in the flesh and give themselves over entirely to the service of men, establishing thus the possibility of their progress and sanctity unto the realization of the "perfect man," which means the fully mature man.[12]

For the attainment of this maturity, specifically priestly, one must see as indispensable the total gift of one's self not only to God and to Christ, but also to the faithful, to one's own local Church and to the Church universal. The priest must consider himself an *oblation* even as did Christ. He must pattern himself upon the Christ of the cross (there is no other known to Christian theology or to history), to the suffering Church (again, there is no other known to history or to theology), and there is no true priest without the cross and suffering at the heart of his life and the heart of his ministry.

In the decree *Presbyterorum Ordinis* the Council clearly affirms, with no little force: "Christ, whom the Father sanctified and consecrated, and sent into the world, 'gave himself for us that he might redeem us from all iniquity and cleanse for himself an acceptable people, pursuing good works' (Titus 2, 14)."[13] "Since in their own measure priests participate in the office of the apostles, God gives them the grace to be ministers of Christ Jesus among the people. They shoulder the sacred task of the gospel, so that the offering of the people can be made acceptable through the sanctifying power of the Holy Spirit. For, through the apostolic proclamation of the gospel, the People of God is called together and assembled so that when all who belong to this People have been sanctified by the Holy Spirit, they can offer themselves as 'a sacrifice, living, holy, pleasing to God' (Romans 12). Through the ministry of priests, the spiritual sacrifice of the faithful is made

---

12 **Presbyterorum Ordinis**, n. 12.
13 **Ibid.**, n. 12.

perfect in union with the sacrifice of Christ, the sole Mediator. Through the hands of priests and in the name of the whole Church, the Lord's sacrifice is offered in the Eucharist in an unbloody and sacramental manner until He Himself returns."[14]

In the twelfth section of the same decree the Council drives home this point once again: "And so it is that they are grounded in the life of the Spirit while they exercise the ministry of the Spirit and of justice, as long as they are docile to Christ's Spirit, who vivifies and leads them. For by their everyday sacred actions themselves, as by the entire ministry which they exercise in union with the bishop and their fellow priests, they are being directed toward perfection of life." Furthermore, the self-giving of the priest, the oblation of himself, of his entire life and all his energies, is continually renewed in the daily Eucharistic celebration of the paschal mystery of Christ and becomes the foundation of the efficacious pastoral action of his priestly ministry: "Priestly holiness itself contributes very greatly to a fruitful fulfilment of the priestly ministry. True, the grace of God can complete the work of salvation even though unworthy ministers. Yet ordinarily God desires to manifest His wonders through those who have been made particularly docile to the impulse and guidance of the Holy Spirit. Because of their intimate union with Christ and their holiness of life, these men can say with the Apostle: 'It is now no longer I that live, but Christ lives in me' (Galatians 2, 20)."[15]

There is no point in denying that at the present moment in history we find ourselves confronted by a certain *infantilism,* psychical, moral, spiritual, sometimes even intellectual in the sense that this includes one's personal interests, even among priests. But the true modern priest, the mature and genuinely fulfilled priest, is, as always, *faithful* to his promises, to the obligations assumed at ordination, to the vocation which placed him in the ranks of the priesthood, provided only he responded to that presumed vocation

---

14 **Ibid.,** n. 2.
15 **Ibid.,** n. 12.

with the self-knowledge, self-discipline and self-giving that we have been discussing. As faithful even as was St. Paul: "Let a man so account us, as servants of Christ and stewards of the mysteries of God. Now here it is required in stewards that a man be found trustworthy" (1 Corinthians 4, 1-2),

Such is the priest who truly knows his own nature and mission, whatever the civilization around him and the culture through which he attained his self-knowledge; such is the priest whose loving act of self-oblation was made with self-discipline, whatever the techniques, consistent with the Gospel, that he achieves his self-discipline and his abnegation for Christ. Thus does he express, as did his predecessors in the priesthood over the centuries, that fidelity which, in the eyes of the world, has always identified him as an authentic, ordained witness to Christ, distinct but not separate from his brethren in the Christian community, realizing the paschal mystery, diffusing the love of the Father for mankind, mankind called to share the dignity of the Son of God, the heritage of God as a co-heir with Christ, maturely, perseveringly, totally. Thus, and only thus, is formed, in the words of Paul, "the mature measure of the fullness of Christ" (Ephesians 4, 13).

The mature man, certainly the mature priest has for his hallmark fidelity to Christ and the Church. This is the reason for his poise and his joy in the Lord, a joy that extends to all things earthly and eternal.

Intellectual maturity, spiritual maturity and pastoral maturity represent, then, indispensable conditions for the genuine and profound renewal of the post-conciliar Church. How could such renewal be achieved on shifting sands and in the midst of the winds that blow in every direction those who have no firm roots in self-knowledge, self-discipline and self-giving?

VII

The Resurrection: Fact or Myth?

All over the world and almost every day people are revealing one or another hang-up about the faith.

Some of these difficulties pertain to precepts of the Christian moral code. Others touch on dogmas of the Christian creed, including its sources in the authoritative witness of the Church and in the claims of Christ Himself. All the points challenged, whether doctrinal or moral, involve "hard sayings" among the teachings of Christ in His Church, like the "hard saying" concerning the presence of Christ in the Eucharist which prompted some of his earliest followers to exclaim: "This is more than we can stomach! Why listen to such words?" And they walked no more with Him, the Gospel declares (cf. John 6, 52-69).

The Paschal mystery is one of Christ's "hard sayings" which many of His present day disciples find "hard to stomach," an intolerable burden on human reason, impossible of acceptance.

From the first days of reflection on the mystery of Christ's coming among us, men have found the central event of that mystery, His Resurrection, a stumbling block, and have attempted to "talk it away." St. Matthew's Gospel records one of the first such efforts. Faced with the fact of an empty tomb, the enemies of Christ contrived this explanation: "Say that His disciples came by night and stole the body while we were asleep" (Matthew 28, 13).

Side by side with ready and literal acceptance of the Resurrection through all centuries since the first Easter, stand attempts to explain or to explain away the Scripture story. The approaches vary. They range from radical views like those of Ernest Renan and Frederick Strauss, which reduce the Resurrection to the result of subjective visions in the excited minds of emotionally exhausted disciples, to the milder current discussions concerning the nature of a "historical event" when faith or feeling are involved.

We are told, for example, that the Resurrection of Jesus is a "myth" in a somewhat special sense of the word. It is argued that the story of the raising of Jesus reflects influences of Oriental mythologies about many ancient divinities. It is related of these that they had suffered the human fate of death but had triumphantly risen again from the dead.

What do we mean when we say that Christ has risen, literally and historically, from the dead? For one thing, such a claim runs counter to human experience. Perhaps the Gospel accounts should be seen as symbolic. Perhaps, as some assert, His followers, as a community of charity and good deeds, in carrying on Christ's work with lively love inspired by Him, renew the life by which He went about doing good and thus become a Risen Christ. Might we not say, with such scholars as Rudolf Bultmann, that the Resurrection "is an expression of man's conviction that the origin and the purpose of the world in which he lives are to be sought not within it but beyond it . . . ", without getting bogged down in speculations about a body brought back to physical life? For many, even among "practicing" Christians, this seems sufficient since it enables them to get on with the work (which, they point out, matters most) rather than worry about details of dogma, even on a doctrine which gives the work its point, its sustaining power and its sure direction.

Perhaps the Resurrection of Christ is more an expression of the force of His personality, His spiritual influence which transcends all barriers, even death itself, and which does not depend, it is suggested, on physical or bodily presence. Even after Calvary, could not His captivating and luminous personality live on in Christ's followers through their ardent faith in Him and in His mission? Why not just as well say that this is His Resurrection and that He is, therefore, still with us? Had He not said that wherever two or three would be gathered in His name, there He would be in their midst?

Perhaps a "cosmic Christ" of eventual human perfection is meant when we speak of the Easter event, rather than the physical person of Jesus of Nazareth. After all, Christ did accomplish the mission of setting men on their way to a higher social consciousness and a more sublime understanding and eventual perfection of human nature. Need we constantly rely so on the figure of the Son of Mary resurrected in the flesh? Perhaps the account of the Resurrection of the Galilean as a historical event is only for the "crowd," for their consolation and strengthening, while the "enlightened" may understand its meaning from a higher viewpoint proportionate to their greater intellectual sophistication and spiritual sensitivity. And so, why need we insist that Christ has literally risen from the dead?

Saint Paul took to writing against these views—ever with us, never new—in his earliest letters to the Corinthians. He was clearly appalled by the prospects for the faith and the very lives of Christians if full awareness and acceptance of the historical fact of the physical Resurrection of Jesus were to be forfeited or even diminished. "He has appeared to Cephas, and afterwards to the twelve. Then He appeared to over five hundred of our brothers at once, most of whom are still alive, though some have died. Then He appeared to James and afterwards to all the apostles" (I Corinthians 15, 5-8).

Saint Paul clearly understood that the Person to Whom the Church prays and in Whom Christians believe is Christ the Lord, enthroned in great power and majesty, but Paul well knew that his Lord is the same Jesus of Nazareth Who was crucified and now is risen, risen in a manner that not merely compels faith but convinces eyewitnesses.

The other early followers of Jesus proclaimed Him Lord even as do we. It is precisely because of the Resurrection that they did so, as it is because of the Resurrection that we do so. We cannot make a distinction between the Lord Who is God and Jesus Who is Man. The faith of the apostles, as ours, says that Jesus, the Carpenter, is Christ the Risen Lord. He is gone into the kingdom of death and emerged again the same Person, not a phantasm, not a being so transformed but what He is still identical with the Jew Whose accents Magdalen knew, still recognized by gestures familiar to His friends, as, for example, in the breaking of bread (cf. Luke 24, 35) .He is God's Son with new clarity, but still Mary's flesh.

Saint John, who had multiple titles to trustworthiness in identifying the Master, recounts the glory of the Risen Lord in the grand apocalyptical, "I am the beginning and the end, the first and the last, the alpha and the omega" (Apocalypse 1, 8). But it is no "mythical" personality to whom he refers, no ideal "cosmic Christ" yet to be. The eyes of the Risen Lord are those that looked at him so many times, the feet are those that had walked many miles with him in Palestine, the voice is that same voice he heard and loved so often. This is Jesus. It is the Jesus of the Last Supper close to Whom he had eaten, the Jesus of Calvary Whose agonies he had witnessed and Whose provisions for His Mother's care he would implement. And this Jesus is the Lord. The Jesus of history and the Christ of faith are one. And that is what our faith proclaims. "He is risen as He said."

True, John had heard (even as had the others) the pledge of His mystical presence, even to the end of time, among those who would gather in His name. But he had also heard the promises of the renewed physical presence of His Master, restored from death after three days, and it is this promise that John proclaims as fulfilled at Easter.

Our faith illumines us not with *how* this all came to be, but only with the *what* and the *why* of the events of the first Easter. We are required, if we be Christians in any full sense, to believe that Christ is risen even as He said He would be. We are told this as a fact and asked to hold it in faith. For only faith can make sense out of this Easter event. There is no possibility nor point in God's plan of knowing how this Israelite of Galilee could rise conquering death. No science, no intellectual insight can yield the faith to which the witnesses of that fact lay claim when they testify: Christ is risen.

"I have seen the Lord." Mary Magdalen ,in the garden of the empty tomb, saw the Lord and so testified to the apostles and to the early Church; through them she testifies to all subsequent Christians. Those five words, the original good news, contain the essential message of Christianity. For the believer the testimony handed down from generation to generation gives rise to faith sufficient for each also to say Christ is risen. Jesus rose and, therefore, men believe in Him, strive to do His Will, and seek to identify with Him by faith in His teaching and imitation of His deeds. So has it been since the garden of Easter, since Emmaus, since the Cenacle, since Pentecost—and all because of things seen, heard, touched, known.

Jean Guitton, in his book, *Jesus: The Eternal Dilemma,* sums up this point of fact and logic. "The first articles of faith, the first hymns to Christ in a just beginning liturgy, the words of Saint Paul and the other writers in the New Testament Epistles, the deeds of the apostles as recorded in the Book of the Acts, the observations of the Roman magistrates—these all assure us of the fact that the first followers worshipped Jesus, adored Him, and that, in these often divided communities comprised of Jews and pagans, there was no argument at all on this point. It was Jesus Who was risen."

It is frequently pointed out that the New Testament biblical writers were not trying to write documented scientific history or systematic biography. It is said that their writings were, in an honest sense, "propaganda," enthusiastic proclamations. All this is true enough, but we must not be misled by such descriptions. Enthusiasm is not its own source. This "propaganda" was the work of conscientious men supremely concerned with serving and spreading *truth;* their enthusiasm was not in a vacuum or directed toward an abstraction. It was a response to a *fact* involving a *person*.

The *fact* was precisely the Resurrection; the *person* was Jesus Christ, Whose Risen Life they proclaimed with the same fervor and conviction as they proclaimed His death. It was not an abstraction that died on the cross. Nor was it a ghost that rose from the dead. The witnesses to both events were the same. This *fact* is set forth thus by Saint Paul: "First and foremost, I handed on to you the facts which have been imparted to me: that Christ died for our sins, in accordance with the Scriptures; that He was buried; that He was raised to life on the third day, according to the Scriptures" (I Corinthians 15, 3, 4). A special solemnity was attached to the truth of this fact by Paul: "If there be no Resurrection, then Christ was not raised; and if Christ was not raised, then our Gospel is null and void, and so is your faith" (I Corinthians 15, 12). Nothing could be more candid, more clear, more cogent.

/ For us the Resurrection is, then, not simply one among many articles of faith; it is the heart of the matter, the beginning of the Christian experience, the cornerstone of the Christian creed, the central premise of Christian liturgical cult. We believe it on the witness of others, as men do all things that they believe. But for those chosen in God's Providence to be the witnesses whom we believe, the Resurrection was an objective experience. They not only believed, they *saw* the Lord. Their testimony was to a fact and to a fact that gives origin, purpose and substance to everything we mean by Christianity.

The Scriptural texts are without ambiguity. The object of their testimony does not rest on the vague affirmation that Christ is alive, somehow, somewhere, but directly and concretely on the physical reality of a resurrected body, the body of a Person they well know and recognize.

Cardinal Daniélou, facing up to the question of whether we have here a "myth" or a reality in his recent work *La Résurrection,* flatly states the issue: "The word resurrection does not have two senses. Either it signifies that the body of Christ lay no longer in the tomb, but was alive by the power of God and, therefore, able to be unmistakably identified as He always had been by the witnesses—or it signifies nothing." It is at this point that the precision of the witnesses takes on great seriousness. They invoke the words of the Risen Christ Himself to express and confirm their certainty: "See my hands and my feet. Touch Me and see, no ghost has flesh and bones as you can see that I have. Place your fingers here, see My hands; reach your hand here and put it into My side, be not unbelieving but believe" (John 20; 27, 28).

The apostles and their disciples are the witnesses of the Risen Lord, not first because they believed, but because they *saw* Him and therefore believed. It is on account of their testimony, transmitted to us by the living Church, that we believe. In the same sense that the apostles are the witnesses to all that Jesus said and did in Judea and Jerusalem that they are the witnesses to the Resurrection and its results (Acts of the Apostles 10, 34-41).

It is this view of the testimony of the disciples concerning the Risen Christ that sustains us when some question the historicity of the accounts of the Resurrection. Despite the enthusiasm of the Evangelists and their intense commitments, the narrative of the Resurrection still remains history. The loving faith of the authors of the Gospels does not annul the historical value of the events they felt obliged to proclaim. The fact that they related these events with joyful fervor should confirm rather than call into question the reality of what they saw. The confrontation with the Risen Christ is the fact that the Gospels are intent on relating; the testimony to the Resurrection had this fact as its point of departure.

Concerning the reliability of the Gospels as historical documents, recent studies have, if anything, confirmed their basic historicity. Common to them all is the one tradition, in various forms, that Jesus proclaimed the Kingdom of God, was crucified, died, was buried and rose again on the third day.

If asked what happened on Easter morning the convert Paul,

the ardent John, the doubting Thomas, the discouraged pilgrims to Emmaus, the faithful women, the temperamental Peter, all the diverse company of the infant Church would have replied not in terms of the mystery of *how* but in terms merely of *what* they knew as facts: We saw an empty tomb; we saw the Risen Lord; we talked with Him, walked with Him, planned with Him—and we now bear witness to all this for all mankind.

For the *why* of the Resurrection we must turn to the meditative passages, the theology, so to say, of Scripture, as distinct from the passages recording events. Christ is risen and in the mystery of His person lies the answer to what the Resurrection means for those who believe in Him.

Saint Paul explains to the Corinthians and Romans that Christ's Resurrection is a pledge of our own life to come in an immortality as personal as that of Christ and an eventual resurrection as real. It is through the Resurrection of Christ that the human body finds its place in God's great plan for redemption and in the Catholic tradition of Christian Humanism. "If the Spirit of Him Who raised Jesus from the dead dwells within you, then the God Who raised Jesus Christ from the dead will also give new life to your mortal bodies through His indwelling Spirit" (Romans 8, 11).

This is the Christian premise for the rejection of all Manicheism, Jansenism, Puritanism or like heresies which see the body as irredeemably evil, mere dirt or otherwise debased—heresies the names and historic forms of which we do well continually to recall if we are not forever to repeat their errors and endure their evils. It is also the foundation of the Christian Humanism which accepts all God's gifts, above all life, as good and disposes us to exercise purposeful and fruitful dominion over them.

The Resurrection is also our release from fear. It was in anticipation of this victory that Christ bade His followers to fear not, since He had overcome the world. Above all, the believer in the Resurrection is freed from fear of death. Nor is his fearlessness the forlorn courage of the Stoic; it is warm with the promise of the traditional preface of the Mass for the dead: "In the same Christ the hope of a blessed resurrection has dawned for us, bringing all who are under the certain, sad sentence of death the consoling promise of future immortality. For those who have been faithful, life is not ended but merely changed, and when this earthly abode dissolves, an eternal dwelling place awaits them in heaven."

This hope has its firm foundation on the fact that Christ is risen. The Father Who raised up Jesus pledges in and through Jesus His life-giving power to the bodies of all who die, as did Jesus, obedient to His Will. It is the work of His Spirit to prepare us for the day when the Resurrection will accomplish in each of us, if we be faithful, all that God did for our Elder Brother and our Lord.

This will be finally and universally achieved at the Lord's return in final judgment. But in the meantime the Spirit of life works within the soul of each of us: "We are citizens of heaven and from heaven we expect our deliverer to come, the Lord Jesus Christ. He will transfigure the body belonging to our humble state, and give it a form like that of His own resplendent body, by the very power which enables Him to make all things subject to Himself" (Philippians 3, 21).

By His death He would be glorified, said Jesus, and, through Him, we also. "The hour has come for the Son of Man to be glorified. In truth, I tell you, a grain of wheat remains a solitary grain unless it falls into the ground and dies, but if it dies it becomes a rich harvest" (John 12; 23, 24). It is for this reason that Jesus' death is a glorification; His life is given up, offered in sacrifice through His death, in order that it may have a permanent, redeeming effect. He sought to win by His death a new life for all men and the first fruit of that new life is His own Resurrection.

Through His Resurrection Christ releases in history and to all men the Spirit of God. This Spirit, the Spirit of Truth and of Love, gives Life to all men who accept Him.

109

"The words that I have spoken to you are spirit and life" (John 1, 1-14). The Resurrection is the act by which that life-giving Spirit is let loose in the world. So we are not only confronted in the Resurrection of Christ with a pledge of a life to come, but we are given clues as to the manner of our share in the life of God's life-giving Spirit. But all these hints of the *why* of the Resurrection depend on the *fact* that Jesus is risen.

When we say "I believe in Jesus Christ Who rose again from the dead . . . and in the Resurrection of the body and the life of the world to come," we are only repeating what the author of the Apocalypse meant years earlier, "Jesus is the living one . . . I died and behold I live forevermore" (Apocalypse 2, 8).

Paul Claudel, writing on the Resurrection of the body, speaks of how, by His Resurrection, Jesus makes the continuity of this life and the life of the world to come clear to our mortal eyes: "Human life will continue. Our Savior's asurance is formal: There where I am, you also will be. Our life after death will thus be His life. In the world beyond we shall not be exiled; there will be no radical change. We shall pass from the world of effects to the world of cause. Instead of seeing reality in terms of its effects, we shall see it—in God—in terms of cause."

There are other implications in the *why* of the Resurrection, especially for an age that speaks so frequently of "meaning," and "value," of "personal worth" and "human dignity." With the Resurrection of Christ, the whole perspective of life is changed. Man can now look at a world and a humanity great with meaning not only in itself as the result of its divine creation but also in its re-creation by a redemption and renewal not less divine; the Christian can see all creation, above all its human stewards, against the horizon of the ultimate realities of a life to come as well as against those of its own space-time validities.

With what our elders in the faith used to call "the perspective of eternity," we can approach each day, its vexations, its joys, its threatening problems and its fleeting consolations. We have here no lasting city; but, whatever our worth, our dignity, our value, it is immeasurable increased when we see it in the light of a life to come that knows no end. What an irony it would be if human life, so rich with promise, so limitless in its hopes, so determined to survive in the face of whatever outrage or affliction, were confined within the tragic dimensions of a body that begins to die at birth.

Gabriel Marcel once spoke with great force to this point, "The world today can be endured only if one's spirit is riveted on this hope in the Resurrection. For us Christians living today something especially influences us to believe in the resurrection of the body: it is, for example, what we know the body endured in the concentration camps. One feels that human flesh has undergone such intolerable outrage that it must receive some kind of reparation in glory. . . . I believe life today is unendurable if one's spirit is not rooted in the hope of our creed. If this hope were shared by a greater number, perhaps a respect for the flesh and for the body, so terribly lacking in our time, would be restored."

Marcel's reflection suggests new (and intensely relevant) points for contemporary meditation on the fuller theological content and social message of Saint Paul's insistence that those who suffer with Christ, not only in spirit but even in their bodies, are destined to share the glory of His Resurrection: "For I reckon that the sufferings of this time are not worthy to be compared with the glory to come, that shall be revealed in us" (Romans 8, 16-18). "Always bearing about in our body the mortification of Jesus, that the life also of Jesus may be made manifest in our bodies. . . . "

To a world permeated by relativism, the Resurrection, set forth as an historical fact, stands for a complex of values based on absolutes. To an age beset with fear, doubt, and rumors of worse things yet to come, the Resurrection heralds a joyous triumph over death, a victory over time, but also the reality of justice and a judgment to come. It is an anchor of steady mooring in a world buffeted by the waves of relativism, lack of vision, even despair.

111

Those in suffering, in frustration, in abandon, the Resurrection consoles with the hope by which Job in the Old Testament was sustained. "This I know, that my Avenger lives and he, the Last, will take his stand on earth. After my awakening, he will set me close to him, and from my flesh I shall look on God" (Job 19: 25, 26).

Ours is a generation frequently close to tears, often short on joy. Its mood is that of the melancholy disciples described by Saint Luke in what I, at least, have always found one of the most touching and persuasive of all the passages in Scripture. They were crushed by the crucifixion and burial of Jesus. They are described as sad, men who used to hope but no longer do. Their hope was restored when Jesus Himself joined them on their journey and they returned to Jerusalem saying: "The Lord is risen indeed, and hath appeared to Simon" (Luke 24, 13-34).

In a day and to a culture similarly diminished in hope and tempted to forfeit faith itself, the Church, remembering the Resurrection, sings its Easter refrain: "This is the day that the Lord has made; let us rejoice and be glad in it." And we, with joy restored and faith re-born, echo Saint Paul: "Rejoice, again I say it, rejoice!" For Christ, indeed, is risen and has obtained for us new life.

VIII
Justice Exalts

"Justice exalteth a nation; but sin makes nations miserable."

(Proverbs 14, 34)

The American bishops and priests of whom I am a representative are many, most of them are unknown, certainly unsung by the present generation. Some of them were buried in publicity, some were buried in obscure silence. They took their stands in various periods of crisis within the Church on occasion, within the national community more often, within local communities most often of all. There were perhaps never as many "speaking out" as there should have been, but there were certainly more than we priests and bishops of the Hierarchy are usually given credit for. They were, as they still are, in overwhelming majority themselves the sons of working men and of working men's wives, but they were not chaplains, as men like them must never be chaplains, in class warfare or in intergroup hatreds of any kind.

Those of them who persevered in the struggle, whose work, in fact, bore fruit, who held apparent frustration and useless praise or lack of it in equal realistic regard, were primarily the sons of the Church, seeking to apply her teaching and therefore to follow their consciences. They were Americans, by birth or by naturalization, and so America was the immediate fields of their efforts at reform or progress. But they were Catholics, with the letter "C" in both lower and upper case, and so their concern was with the human family everywhere, as is that of the Universal Church. The human family, the only race of which they admitted the existence, was not for them an abstraction; it meant every person, any person, each person, all persons, the person, wherever he may be, whatever be his background, whichever his color, his condition, his creed, his calling.

I would be unprepared to categorize with the fashionable labels of the hour these men of God who have served the cause of social justice, and therefore of working people in the United States. I have no idea whether they were liberals or conservatives, pragmatists or classicists. Some of them were pastoral-types; some of them were scholars. I only know for certain that they were Catholic, with a capital "C" and a lower case "c," and that like their counterparts in the tremendous social movements of world Protestantism and age-old Judaism people with truly catholic minds and hearts (I am using here the small "c" on the word catholic) they would reject imprisonment and defy classification within any of these largely meaningless and usually vituperative categories so beloved by our contemporary shorthand journalism or hit and run reporting.

Most of them were men like Cardinal Gibbons and Archbishop Ireland, like Bishop Haas and the Spaldings, like Monsignor John Ryan and Father Ray McGowan, each of these being very *cautious,* which means, I suppose, "conservative" in what pertains to the Faith, and each *forward-looking* in what pertains to social action and reform,—which means, I suppose, "liberal." In fact, in all things they were merely trying to be decent, which means faithful in conscience to the teachings of the Church and faithful in service to the needs of God's people.

While I was bishop of Pittsburgh I often wondered whether a priest like, say, Pittsburgh's Father Jimmy Cox felt more at home during the march which he led on Washington, D.C., for social justice or during the pilgrimages which he led to Saint Anne de Beaupre in Canada or to Lourdes in France and to Rome for the rekindling of the ancient Faith of himself and his people! When do you decide to classify him in some subcategory of Catholics? Was it when you found him preaching the need for better wages or housing in order to lead a more humane life? Or was it when

114

you found him reproducing the Holy Stairs and preaching the traditional doctrines of penance, prayer and basic Faith by which even the most human of decent lives is lifted to the level of the Divine?

And if you have this problem in classifying the Catholic clergy and bishops who bore their witness to social justice and human dignity, in season and out, with or without success, ending as they began, fully the servants of the people and yet faithfully bound to the altar, I must remind you that you will have the same problem classifying Protestant Christian or prophetic Hebrews who have used their ministry in behalf of the social gospel or the social witness of the Hebrew prophets—but have never forgotten what are the credal premises in faith of that witness, what is the secret of the hope that the world can be renewed and the conviction that the world continually needs renewal from outside itself. On this, Jew, Protestant and Catholic have been in agreement from the ten commandments, to the collective pastorals of the various Boards of Bishops or rabbinates, from the encyclicals of the Popes on social and moral questions to the most recent local declaration issued in agreement under ecumenical auspices.

Those secrets are simple. They are set forth in the text that I read to you this morning. The hope that society can be redeemed and renewed is in the word *justice,* of which God is the author and which is one of His attributes. The source of our confusion, our embarrassment, or all our moral and social evil is *sin,* of which Satan is the source and which constitutes his very essence.

Now that you have kindly saluted me by including me among those who have tried to keep this message of Sacred Scripture alive in the battle for human progress, let me come to my second, most important and final point. Nothing substantial, permanent or truly positive can be accomplished about any of the problems which so beset and bewilder us—the problems of war, the problems of infidelity (whether within the family unit by double timing, within the nation by treachery, within the Church by apostasy), the problems of maldistribution of the resources and

115

the wealth of the world, the problem of hunger, the problem of unemployment, the problem of genocide, whether by gas chamber or by government programmed contraception, the problem of neglect, whether it reveals itself in illiteracy or delinquency or mere pollution of the air—nothing can be done about any of these problems until we stop using technical jargon and sweet talk—Al Smith used to call it using words to conceal meanings—and put proper labels on things where those labels are called for.

As one speaking in the biblical and religious traditions of the Judeo-Christian world, for example, I suggest that we begin with the return to our vocabularies of the word and above all to our convictions of the concept "sin." I suggest that if our nation is miserable, or largely so despite its affluence and its blessings, if our world is, in fact, clearly miserable in the news reports despite its infinite resources and capacity for happiness; if our beloved city, to be quite specific, is miserable this weekend despite all the imaginative forces at work in its "renaissance" and all its financial power to build so ambitiously and so beautifully—if all this is true, and it is, then something essential is missing from among its assets and something vicious is present among its liabilities. The first of these is frequently mentioned, though with what degree of conviction I am never entirely sure. That something is *justice, the justice that exalts a nation, a church, a city, a family, a community.* That justice is clearly missing somewhere along the line, however loudly it is invoked on every side.

But the vicious thing that is *present* and that *no one ever mentions*—or mentions *only reluctantly* and as if he were crudely introducing a discredited concept into an otherwise intelligent discussion—that something is the fact of *sin.*

The present miserable condition that surrounds us is visible all over the city, all over the nation, all over the world. Yet no one seems willing to brave the spirit of the times by pronouncing the word which sums it up and explains it. The reason for this reluctancy is that the misery is present within these very walls because it is present within our very hearts, deep in our hearts. It is the more difficult to eradicate precisely because we will not say the word and admit what it means and how alone it can be purged.

Whatever may be the secondary and complicating causes, the plain fact is that the city, the nation, the world, and, if you will, the Church, is not made miserable by maladjustment, mal-distribution, maladministration, misinformation—but by *sin*.

We must not be simplistic or rabble-rousing in this matter, charged with the emotions and vocabulary of a camp revival meeting. Nor, on the other hand, must we abjectly conform to the spirit of the moment and limit ourselves to its vocabulary and text book jargon. We need not become hermits, in pious flight from positive action; that, all by itself, would be no solution to the social question. Neither must we become religious fanatics, denouncing the values of the world or the wisdom of its programs; that could easily become heresy, another word we would do well to restore to our vocabulary and our convictions.

But we must restore something of the proportion presently so gravely violated when the word "sin" rarely appears in a public pronouncement, and then usually as a figure of speech, and never appears in a purportedly serious analysis of the true causes of our problems. The use of the words "sin" and "repentance" have seemed almost artificial, when used by public authorities at all, since the death of Woodrow Wilson—and increasingly, even pronouncements put out by religious agencies appear more concerned with the positive, creative support of sociological and political programs—a support in fact frequently needed and too often with-held—than with prophetic denunciation of the fact of sin or prophetic calls to effective repentance.

Instead, even religious spokesmen offer such specific suggestions, they are such as any common sense group, speaking with the wisdom of the world, should come up with, while the prophetic denunciation of sin, specific and unashamed, together with the

117

call to conversion, specifically to God and by the mercy and grace of God, are either muted, or omitted, or wrapped up in rhetoric seemingly designed to reduce the concept of sin and the nature of conversion to some sort of broad consensus in which God is allowed and His Church accepts only a constitutional voice, certainly when the problem is thought of as secular and political, and even when it is acknowledged to pertain to faith and morals.

The justice that exalts a nation is not the justice of a constitutional deity; it is the justice of the God of the Bible. The sin that makes a nation miserable is the sin denounced by Isaiah and the prophets, by Jesus, by the independent papacy. The sin, or the concept of sin arrived at by consensus, determined in the light of widespread habit, public policy or cultural *mores* at any given moment, may tranquilize a nation, undermine a nation, and, by definition, be acceptable to a nation. *But it may still be the sin that makes a nation miserable.*

Let me be more specific. During the last several years spokesmen for various church and ecumenical groups in America have put out sincere, eloquent and well-intentioned statements on social questions. Some of these have been concerned with peace and war. Some have been concerned with poverty and what to do about it. Some have been linked to intergroup disorders in the cities or starvation in rural areas. Some have been linked to special seasons, to Peace Day for example, or to Labor Day. I have had a hand in the writing of a few of these and so I know the earnestness, the desire to be of service, the careful thought that goes into the preparation of most of them.

Some of them discuss the symptoms of our miserable condition. They lament the violence which is the most obvious and most painful of the symptoms of our miserable condition which they record as would a clinical report. Some of them seek to explore more profound levels of the causes of these symptoms, the roots of our misery. Not a few even suggest specific remedies, particularly in terms of cash, allotment of monies, improved programming, new approaches to tired or discredited political, religious, community or private efforts to relieve the symptoms and to remove the only causes which are mentioned. These causes are invariably economic, political, social, cultural, geographical, or historical—but sin is stamped all over them. Yet *sin* is rarely if ever mentioned, let alone acknowledged.

If only because I am standing in a pulpit—but I would do the same if I were talking in Congress, at a Labor Union Convention, or at a roundtable on social problems,—I feel bound to emphasize the fact of *sin*—to declare the presence of *sin* among us; to suggest that it is *sin* which makes a nation, a family, or a city, miserable; that *sin* is at the heart of all the problems to which we give such attention as we give the misery around us; that repentance from *sin* is essential to the correction of those problems; that unless *sin* is acknowledged and repented our social problems are, in fact, insoluble, our misery is indefinite, how much the sin may be buried in our subconscious, put out of our minds, or whatever else is meant by the phrase "swept under the rug."

Our Labor Day statements mention justice; they nowhere mention sin. They underline, in positive and intelligent fashion, the need to face up to the causes of social unrest and the need to confront the causes of poverty; the Church is specifically urged to attack those causes, largely in terms of the indispensable practical strategies admittedly needed to attack the problems which have economical, political or social consequences and complications. But even the enumeration of the causes which the Church is specifically called upon to confront does not mention that radical cause which the Church is primarily and uniquely instituted to confront, charged by Its Founder to confront, inspired by its saints to confront, called by Its God to confront: namely, the radical, all-pervading fact of sin that makes a nation miserable.

The Church is an institution that works in the world. As such it must cooperate with all other institutions honestly engaged in fighting whatever problems impede human progress, threaten hu-

119

man life, limit human freedom and pervert happiness here below, while destroying the possibility of these in the life of the world to come. But the supreme business of the Church is the prophetic, moral leadership proclamation that certain of the problems which so curtail life here below and threaten it hereafter are not merely economic, nor political, nor cultural, nor social, nor ill advised labor or education policies—*they are objectively sinful.* In the words of the otherwise often doubtful Dutch Catechism, sin is the refusal to love others or the Other, by which the Dutch Catechism, since it spells the "Other" with a capital "O," presumably means God; therefore, sin is the refusal to love others and to love God.

Christ worded it a little more simply. He declared sin to be the refusal to obey God's Law and He defined God's Law in terms of Love. He said that we are guilty of moral evil, by violating God's Law, if we refuse to love the Lord, our God, with our whole mind, our whole heart, our whole soul. Then He added, in effect: "By the same token, you commit the same sin if you refuse to love your neighbor the way you love yourselves—if you refuse your neighbor the same opportunity to be, to grow, to be free, to work, to join up in the movements designed to protect basic rights—such as life, liberty and the opportunity for work—that your love for yourself prompts you to establish for yourself and guarantee for yourself."

It is as simple as that. When all the technical jargon, the history courses, the sociology studies, the research projects, the government reports and the convention resolutions have made their suggestions and played their part, it is still the Sacred Scripture that has the final say: *Justice exalts a nation; but sin makes nations miserable.*

The Bible uses the word *sin,* in one or another form, about six hundred times: the Kerner Report does not mention it at all, which is probably defensible in a secular state but is no great help in a miserable society. What is even more lamentable, few other statements of the causes of our misery, except perhaps those of

120

extreme fundamentalists who discredit their witness by religious fanaticism and social myopia, include *sin* either when they list the causes of our misery or attempt to program their solutions; there may be comfortable talk about "change of attitude" but little or no call for repentance, change of heart, in the strict biblical and traditional, theological sense.

I need hardly say that, except in terms of sin, the Bible never uses most of the words that are used to describe the processes, priorities, projects, interfaith programming, ecclesiastical and political budgeting which are the commonplaces of our political and even religious declarations on these matters and approaches to their solutions. It talks about *sin* as a *cause* and *love* as a *cure,* the cure that casts out the fears at the heart of our hatred, our basic *sin.*

I suppose that I am not, certainly in any narrow sense of traditional polemic, "a Bible Christian." My Protestant Christian brethren will understand that I would not believe in "Scripture alone" as the source of faith or morals. I believe that the Scriptures call for very careful interpretation and for divinely-inspired powers of discernment of their message of which I do not feel capable, all by myself. Hence my grateful dependence on the authority of the Church and the word of its apostolic teaching.

Moreover, I have a deep veneration for the power of human intellect, for the ultimate reliability of common sense, for the wisdom of the ages, for all the things of which Dante saw Virgil and natural reason, as well as natural ethic, to be the symbols. And so I know what the American hierarchy meant when, in connection with another moral problem currently disguised and distorted as merely a political worry, medical difficulty and sociological phenomenon, they dared to call the sin of contraception an "objective evil." I also know that even pagans, even atheists, the present moral mess that surrounds us would be called what it is: the proximate result of poverty, of unemployment and discrimination—but the ultimate result of hatred—which is an "objective evil"—which, again, means *sin.*

121

The misery we are worrying about all over the world at the moment—in Pittsburgh and elsewhere at home, in Northern Ireland, in the Middle East, in areas of Africa, in disputed zones of Europe,—is given all manner of names and explanations. In fact, it is usually one or another form of *racism*—which means of *sin*—which means of *hatred*—which means of *fear*. Fear is not cast out by knowledge alone and hatred is not diminished by money or power alone—as many wealthy families well know and some powerful organizations. Fear is cast out by love—and that is what the Church is expected to preach and to give before it opens its mouth or its offices for anything else. *The Church exists to confront sin and communicate love.*

Let me linger for a moment on this concept of *sin,* because this is the heart of the matter and on this you will not hear much, I am afraid, in the discussion of our community tensions. On this point the Dutch Catechism, often too obscure and inaccurate on other matters, is remarkably useful. Discussing the failures of Christians and the nature of sin, it says that the great fault of men is not that some social mechanism is out of order, the way Marxists suppose, but that free will is misused in favor of objective evil. It says further that evil does not ultimately mean just imperfection or disorder that we can straighten out with mere human intelligence and human energy, but that it involves turning away from God, which situation cannot be corrected by man alone. It goes on to say that sin is not merely transgression of some abstract, lofty law, but involves a personal offense against love. Finally, and most importantly, it underscores that sin is not just an offense against man, as secularists and humanists are limited to saying, but it is also and supremely an offense against the Creator and Redeemer of the human race. It is a deliberate offense again Divine and human love, which cannot be repaired by human means, or human solutions to human problems.

Sin is harmful to man, but the point is that as a transgression of God's Law it always involves a refusal to love as God wishes us to love both Him and one another.

That refusal may not always be conscious and fully willed; it admits of degrees of guilt, according to cultural conditioning, fear of heart, confusion of mind, degrees of understanding or of ignorance—again as the American Bishops pointed out in discussing the objective evil that is contraception, and in suggesting the degrees of guilt which may be present in an individual caught up in all the pressures and propaganda, slogans and sneers of a contraceptive civilization, political atmosphere or economic cultural. But the corrosive objective evil is there, all the same, and so is objective sinfulness, just as it was present in the days of slavery in the United States when respectable men, still held in great renown, were, in fact, slaveholders, and as men may be acceptable today in social or diplomatic circles even though they represent nations whose whole economy is based on slavery in one or another form.

I do not pretend to say that George Washington, for example, or Thomas Jefferson, were subjectively sinners, but I do say that the situation of slavery to which they were apparently blind was objectively evil; it was, in fact, sinful, though they may have been kindly men and, for one reason or another, diminished in their guilt.

The same thing goes for racism, which is a form of spiritual slavery as there are forms of cultural imperialism long after political and economical imperialisms have ended their exploitation. Such racism is sinful and it calls for change of attitude, a change of heart, a radical conversion in the Scriptural sense. It is not enough to call it a "disorder," or a "lesser evil," or "a stage in the striving toward a greater ideal"—as some Christians say about life-prevention, abortion or the bombardment of non-combatant villages, or as other Christians say about the discriminations, segregations, exclusions and inequalities at the bottom of our present misery. *It is a sin.* That is *all* it is and it is *no less* than that.

123

The guilt of some involved in it, like that of some of those involved in other sins we have mentioned or could mention, may be understandable because of cultural conditioning; may be pardonable because of invincible ignorance; may be diminished because of panic, fear, confusion or instability—but the situation remains *objectively sinful.* The very first business of the Church, Catholic or Protestant, and of the Synagogue, is to put that fact in clear focus and unmistakable clarity it is facing the causes of poverty and confronting the causes of our misery.

This is the mandate that God Almighty gave the Church and the Synagogues—to preach the fact and the nature of sin as the cause of our misery, the need and the nature of repentance as the beginning of the cure of our problems. To be sure, neither God, nor the prophets, nor Christ left it as that. God Almighty has also given the Church an agenda as to what it is to do about social problems beyond what is the obligation of the State, primary custodian of public order and the temporal common good. He has done this through His Sacred Scriptures, which tell us that a brother helped by a brother makes a strong city; that every field is to be plowed by its owner with a view to what he can make available to the needy; that not those who say "Lord, Lord" but those who keep the Law of God, which is a law of charity, are worthy of the Kingdom; and that the final judgment concerning whether we go to heaven or to hell will depend on what we did for those in prison, who need clothing, food, housing or the plain comfort of our company and moral support. This mandate the Church received from God Almighty before it received volunteer mandates or rebukes from Concerned Citizens, Action Groups or Political Commentators. But this mandate follows upon and depends upon the primary mandate God gave His Church to preach love not hate: to remind men and governments that it is justice which makes a nation powerful and it is sin which makes a nation—or a city—miserable.

The lesson for Labor Day 1969, especially to the Labor

Unions whom we have tried to honor and encourage each year, is too obvious to need explicit declaration. So, let me sum up all I have tried to say by three brief quotes:

1) Of the many sayings attributed to the late President John F. Kennedy one is particularly facile sounding and particularly false. It went to the general effect that there are no human problems which do not admit of human solutions. If this means our present social problems of poverty, violence, war and racism it is flat nonsense, however cheerful. Our only problems worth mentioning are due to sin, particularly hatred, though the sin may be the kind the Old Testament child of God prayed he might be forgiven: from my *unconscious* sins, O Lord, deliver me—from the sins against life, against the dignity of my neighbor, against the common good of which I am not even aware, but which nonetheless objectively ruin Thy divine order! Deliver me, as I beg you to do, from the sins which I admit and which I consciously confess—but do even this by Thy mercy and Thy grace, because I cannot do it alone.

2) In fact, it is these objective evils, these objective sins of which so many of us are sometimes unconscious, because the world tells us that they are not so sinful after all, it is *these* which cause our misery. Pope Pius XII once said: "Perhaps the greatest sin in the world today is that men have begun to lose the sense of sin." This would take another sermon in terms of a few situations within the Church itself. I limit myself to the problems in our general community. We have more sense of what is bad politics, bad diplomacy, bad military tactics, bad medicine, bad technology, bad busineess procedures, bad union interests or bad public relations than we have the sense of what is objectively sinful. We would almost rather have a rogue in charge of our affairs, if he kept trouble away from the door, than a saint if he called us sinners to our faces and told us that we must have a change of heart before we can change the mess around us.

3) My final quotation is from a perhaps surprising source. But it has to do both with the nature of sin and with the contemporary rejection of the whole idea of sin as the cause of our misery, as well as with its opposite as the only ground for our hope. I had never thought that I would quote James Joyce's novel *ULYSSES* from this or any other pulpit. But here goes. Its principle character, a Dublin Jew, is quoted by Joyce as saying to the typical characters in his Dublin hangout: "It's no use," he says, "force, hatred, that's not a life for men and women; insult and hatred is no way of life; everybody knows that it is the very opposite of that, that is really life." "What is?," says Alf, one of the citizens. "It is love," says Bloom, "I mean the opposite of hatred." And they all laughed at him.

I beg you love one another and all God's children. Let us purge our hearts of hatred, which is sin, and thus purge our city of all the misery which hatred begets. Let us not merely love one another *sentimentally;* let us do the *works of love,* the first of which is justice. For it is: *Justice that exalts a nation; but sin that makes nations miserable.*

IX

Faith and Social Action

The Scripture tells us that at a given moment Christ began to do and teach, not one alone, not the other alone, but both together.

In the Church Christ continues to do and to teach. In what spirit, then, does He now urge us to *do* the works of justice? What demands does He make on our fidelity to *HIS teaching?*

In the doing of its works, the Church in our day seems "open" or "forward-looking" in facing social problems. Yet, in her teaching she seems "cautious," or "conservative," especially in matters of faith and morals. Such is the import of the Pastoral Constitution *Gaudium et Spes;* such certainly is the tenor of the *Dogmatic Constitution on the Nature of the Church.*

In like manner, our Holy Father, Pope Paul, like his predecessors from Leo XIII to Pope John, brings to social questions a prevailing "liberal" outlook, a clear openness to the future, the outlook of Pope John's *Mater et Magister* and *Pacem in Terris* or his own *Populorum Progressio* and address to the United Nations. But also like his predecessors, the Pope speaks on doctrinal points with the fidelity of that witness to tradition which is echoed in the Year of Faith *Credo,* the encyclicals *Aeterna Dei Sapientia, Mysterium Fidei* and *Humanae Vitae,* and in Pope Paul's repeated affirmations of the received faith of our fathers.

The contrast recalls a parallel in St. Paul, a parallel which may be instructive for the times. No one can fail to note the openness of St. Paul to the wide and varied world of the Gentiles of his times, to their cultures and to the need for changes in the old order to meet the needs of the new. And yet, St. Paul was intransigent in his fidelity to the revelations made to the prophets and, above all, to the truth proclaimed in and through Christ Jesus.

The present-day seeming contradiction which occurs to me can be stated thus: In our moment of history, both the history of the Church and the history of mankind, a "liberal" social attitude and a "progressive" spirit are the need of the hour. But such openness requires, as an indispensable condition of its health and effectiveness, a jealous regard for doctrinal soundness, an attachment to the faith that is unqualified save for human frailty. I offer the thesis that in a period of social turbulence, indeed revolution, those who are committed to "openness" and needed change on the level of things human are doomed to be blown about by every wind of doctrine unless they have a commitment not less certain to fixed principles of faith and morality.

I am suggesting that it is not only possible but desirable, even necessary, for the prevailing mood of the Church in our day to be one of open, progressive positions on social questions, above all in what pertains to the freedom due to the sons of God, but together with a profound fidelity to the established truth at the heart of religious faith, the faith by which we are, in fact, made free.

With a measure of oversimplification, perhaps, but I trust no injustice to the realities, my thesis is this: *Social openness is the need of the hour: theological caution is not less great the need. Doctrinal integrity is essential to the faith, but it is not less essential to freedom. The faith provides the absolutes against which the relatives of social change are necessarily judged by Christians: absolutes concerning God, the person, the honor of God and the dignity of the person, the value of life and the primacy of the spiritual as Christians must see these always and everywhere.*

Herein lies, one strongly feels, the saving formula for the resolution of the tragic ironies set forth by Bonhoeffer in these words of truth: "The demand for absolute liberty brings men to the depths of slavery. The master of the machine becomes its slave. The creature turns against its creator in a strange reenactment of the Fall. . . . The liberation of man as an absolute ideal leads only to man's self-destruction."

128

At our stage in history the temptations of social conservatism could be perilous to the prospects for human freedom, while those of theological liberalism would be fatal to the substance and the future of divine faith and therefore to the very goals of honest liberalism.

Religious faith, properly accepted and lived, provides the moral climate in which human freedoms have their best chance to survive. The Catholics of Poland proclaimed this to Catherine II of Russia: "We love *liberty* and therefore we love *religion* even more; we are *free* because we love *religion*. We shall not deny our *religion* lest we straightway be deprived of our *liberty*."

Conversely, political and economic freedom should provide the social climate most favorable to responsible and vigorous religious faith.

Hence it turns out, by a curious but persuasive paradox, that social outlooks usually identified as "conservative," certainly those which are "reactionary," by tending to inhibit social growth and personal liberty, impede the common good, even as that good is preserved and fortified by the conservative instinct with respect to the faith, an instinct which keeps one on guard against what Cardinal Newman identified as "liberalism in religion."

And so, social progressivism and theological conservatism, far from being inconsistent, can be mutually supportive. They are logical allies in the face of the present crisis in the Church, the crisis of our culture our political order, our very civilization.

That is why those who love both faith and freedom are always *doubly* concerned when the faith appears to be in jeopardy or the Church, the living presence of the teaching Christ in history, is in whatever peril.

Their preoccupation sometimes expresses itself in language that is anxious; it cannot do otherwise, given the gravity of the issues. But they do not, they cannot, lose heart. They know how much of human history, as well as Christian theology, Cardinal Newman summed up when he said:

"In truth the whole course of Christianity from the first, when we come to examine it, is but one series of troubles and disorders. Every century is like every other and to those who live in it seems worse than all times before it. The Church is ever ailing, and lingers on in weakness, 'always bearing about in the body the dying of the Lord Jesus, that the life also of Jesus might be made manifest in her body.' Religion seems ever expiring, schisms dominant, the light of Truth dim, its adherents scattered. The cause of Christ is ever in its last agony, as though it were but a question of time whether it fails finally this day or another. . . . " (*Via Media,* Vol. I, pp. 354-355).

The Christian answer to all this is, of course, confident hope and sustaining love, but these because of steadfast faith and yet more faith. *"I believe, Lord, help thou my unbelief"* (Mark 9, 23). If Newman described the recurring condition of turmoil in which the Church always finds itself, he pointed out not less clearly the solution. He said: "Doubt and difficulty seem our lot; the simple question is—What is our duty under it? . . . Scripture is quite aware of those difficulties . . . it knows them all; it has provided against them by recognizing them. It says, 'Believe' " (*Essays Critical and Historical,* pp. 244-149).

The problem of *Whom* we shall believe and its solution in Christ, the Divine Teacher, are both seen in the sixth chapter of St. John's Gospel. Again Cardinal Newman is our guide to their understanding:

"After our Lord had declared what all who heard seemed to feel to be a hard doctrine, some in surprise and offence left Him. Our Lord said to the Twelve most tenderly, 'Will ye also go away?' St. Peter promptly answered. No! But observe on what grounds he put it: 'Lord, *to whom* shall we go?' . . .If Christ were not to be trusted, there was nothing in the world to be trusted; and this was a conclusion repugnant both to his reason and to his heart. He had within him ideas of greatness and goodness, holiness and eternity—he had a love of them—he had an instinctive hope and longing after their possession. Nothing could convince him that this unknown good was a dream. Divine life, eternal life, was the object which his soul, as far as it had learned to realize and express its wishes, supremely longed for. In Christ he found what he wanted. . . . He might have misgivings at times; he might have permanent and in themselves insuperable objections; still in spite of such objections, in spite of the assaults of unbelief, on the whole, he saw *that* in Christ which was positive, real and satisfying. He saw it nowhere else. 'Thou,' he says, 'hast the words of eternal life; and we *have believed* and *have* known that Thou are the Christ, the Son of the Living God.' As if he said, 'We will stand by what we believed and knew yesterday—what we believed and knew the day before. A sudden gust of new doctrines, a sudden inroad of new perplexities, shall not unsettle us. We *have* believed, we *have* known: we cannot collect together all the evidence, but this is the abiding deep conviction of our minds. We feel that it is better, safer, truer, more pleasant, more blessed to cling to Thy feet, O merciful Saviour, than to leave Thee. Thou *canst not* deceive us: it is impossible. We will hope in Thee against hope, and believe in Thee against doubt, and obey Thee in spite of gloom.'

"Now what are the feelings I have described but the love of Christ? Thus love is the parent of faith. . . . Love of God led St. Peter to follow Christ, and love of Christ leads men now to love and follow the Church, as His representative and voice" (*Essays Critical and Historical,* pp. 249-252).

In brief, then, Christ offers mankind that truth which makes us free. But we must be tenacious of the faith through which there comes to us that truth which frees if we are to be, as the voice of the times invites us to be, the heirs to liberty and the builders, in responsible freedom, of a more sane and saving order.

In this, too, Newman may well have been prophetic when, on the occasion of his coming to Rome ninety years ago to receive his cardinal's hat, he warned against what he called "the spirit of liberalism in religion." He praised what is good and true in liberal theory generally, "for example, not to say more, the precepts of justice, truthfulness, sobriety, self-command, and benevolence." But he saw this spirit, when loosed from firm attachment to the faith, as prompting a great "apostasy," "one and the same everywhere, (though) in detail, and in character, it varies in different countries." He saw that spirit, already shaping up in his times, as ultimately inconsistent with the recognition of any religions whatever as *true,* all being matters of opinion, never of objective fact. Because of its mischief, "over-spreading, as a snare, the whole earth," Newman made his admittance to the Sacred College the occasion to protest that "never did Holy Church need champions (against this kind of 'liberalism in religion') more sorely than now" (*Biglietto* address).

One wonders what Newman would have said had he lived to see his name and his words invoked in defense of a religious spirit which he found so mischievous and which he repudiated in his own times so pointedly, so passionately, and, on occasion, with such personal suffering ! ! !

Newman's passion for the Church of the Fathers, for the primacy of the papacy, for the witness of hierarchy and laity alike to the faith committed to the Apostles is pre-eminently needed if liberalism in the building of peace, the flourishing of the intellectual life, the recognition and service of the person, the progress of civil rights is to have firm roots in truth from which to flourish and fixed, unyielding standards to guarantee its freedoms.

Newman lamented the theological trend of his times because he feared that it would be the ruin of many souls. But he added: "I have no fear at all that it really can do . . . serious harm to the Word of God, to Holy Church, to our Almighty King, the Lion of the tribe of Judah, Faithful and True, or to His Vicar on earth. *Christianity has been too often in what seemed deadly peril, that we should fear for it any new trial now.* [To offset and survive these] . . . commonly the Church has nothing more to do than to go on in her own proper duties, in confidence and peace. . . . "

What we have thus said about the majestic calm and Christian optimism which the ancient faith inspires, together with the magnanimous, venturesome social action which the new hopes invite, is valid everywhere. Everywhere and always we must *do* with the boldness and generosity of Christ, and *teach* without compromise or confusion the Word of God, still echoed across the ages and throughout the world by the voice of the Church, obedient to Him as is He to the Mind and the Will of His Father in God.

We must repeat these joyful, consoling truths in all seasons and all places. But it is especially appropriate to proclaim them on this occasion and here in Rome, where Christ's own Vicar gives the example of *doing* and *teaching*. It is easy to believe them here where the trophies of the apostles, the memories of the martyrs, all the symbols of the city not lightly called "Eternal," declare the abiding strength of truly human aspirations and the immortal power of divine promises.

Let the words of St. Bernard inspire us here in Rome to deepened identity through the Church with the unchanging Christ Who ultimately changes everything: "Surrounded by a company of single-hearted brethren, what have you to fear? What have you to fear at whose side angels stand and whom Christ leads into battle encouraging his friends with the words, 'Fear not, I have overcome the world'? If Christ is with us, who is against us? You can fight with confidence where you are sure of victory. With Christ and for Christ, victory is certain. Not wounds, nor falls, nor bruises, nor (were it possible) can a thousand deaths rob us of victory, if only we do not forsake the fight. Only by desertion can we be defeated. . . . "—desertion from Christ the Divine Teacher of our faith, Christ the Example of our deeds.

X

The Blessed Vision of Peace

The historic connection between religious idealism and the quest for a peaceful world order is familar; the Sacred Scriptures are full of it. So are the encyclicals of the Popes; it is appropriate and helpful frequently to emphasize it particularly when we meet to summon to the struggle for world peace the energies and ideals of our respective religious traditions.

My own reading of the history of ideals reveals the connection to be aboriginal to the specifically religious story of the Western world. It is not to the world of science nor to the world of scholarship that, in fact, we are indebted for the first explicit steps toward a whole world sharing a good that, though it might and must originate among one or another people, is to be shared by all and peacefully held in common.

The wiset and the best of the ancient philosophers and educators, however sublime the ideal of personal perfection they may have taught, never dare dream of the perfection of society by the realization of human solidarity. Socrates, and the twin genuises who have transmitted to us all that was most perfect in the thought of his age, envisioned no social order more perfect than one still cramped and crippled by tribalism and racial division.

Modern nationalism, to be sure, though it has frequently impeded the progress of our race towards international unity, is a great step from the social chaos of tribalism and toward the order of organic society. But the most cultured of pagan societies were a long way even from this. Aristotle does not even discuss the question of how peace is to be kept between his tiny State and the rest of the human race. Certainly, Aristotle shows no love for war as such; true he insists that "we make war for the sake of peace," a historic declaration, indeed, especially if one recalls how it has caught the political imagination of all Europe—of St. Augustine in his *City of God,* of Dante in his *Monarchy,* and of countless others. But Aristotle still looked on war as inevitable and considered human division into tribal or national groups as the normal and necessary condition of society. So with Plato—the organization of his "Fair City" is a militant organization of fighting-men, and peace has little part in his ideal scheme of things.

But the vision which would have seemed foolishness to the Greeks of old was the strength of the ancient Jews.

It is expressed in the mystical meaning of the very name Jerusalem, the visible sign of the blessed vision of peace.

This is the birth, certainly in the Western world, of the *beata pacis visio*—the mystical Jerusalem—in pilgrimage toward which we push forward about which we ask ourselves whether it is a *douce chimere* or a *blueprint.*

The Jews owed that vision to Revelation. It was religion that made the Jews a nation, and it was the consciousness of their religious vocation that opened to them the vision of internationalism. Whether or not one accepts with us the belief that God personally and literally confines of Ur of the Chaldees to conceive in obscure beginnings a world ideal, a universal society that is still in painful travail, this much is certain: the first line is human literature which indicates a spirit of dissatisfaction with mere nationalism and a desire for a world vision is the line in the Hebrew Scriptures which declares that "the Lord said to Abraham: Go forth out of thy country, and from thy kindred, and out of thy father's house, and come into the land which I shall show . . . and in thee shall all the kindred of the earth be blessed. So Abraham went out as the Lord had commanded him" (Genesis 12, 1-4).

And so, one dares to say that if among the political and social movements of the present time there is one which owes its beginnings to religion, however much it has lost its conscious connection with God, and which is still associated with religion in its very

135

notion, it must be that movement which seeks to realize in the social order a human solidarity transcending lines of national or racial division, establishing a unity among mankind co-extensive with the natural unity in which God created the human family in the beginning.

This dream of a universal order of peace among humans is part of the political heritage we owe the Judaeo-Christian tradition; it is as old as our religious history. It is implicit, as we have seen, in the vocation of Israel and it is echoed in the words of the prophets of Israel, Daniel and Isauias and Osee, even during the long generations in which Israel disciplined herself by religious isolation from the Gentile world precisely in order to keep pure the monotheism that is the ontological basis of one human and humane order. It is the most characteristic social doctrine of the Christian ethic; it is explicit in the social teaching of the New Testament, finding its most unmistakable expression in the words by which St. Paul described the Church of Christ at work as a leaven in the social world, a kingdom "where there is neither Gentile nor Jew, circumcision nor uncircumcision, Barbarian nor Scythian, bond nor free" (Colossians 3, 11).

The Risorgimento in Mazzini's Italy, even at the height of its nationalistic excesses and its professed break with the past, at least did not turn back on the ancient hope of a social order greater than the Sovereign State. Mazzini believed intensely in nationalism, but even he recognized that it is only an element in the larger human whole. The Italian Republicans of the last century were not eager to confess their indebtedness to the religious traditions of their fatherland, but the impartial critic will sense that much indeed of Italy's centuries of Catholic culture is distilled into such passages from Mazzini as this from his *Essay on the Duties of Man*:

"We improve with the improvement of humanity, nor without the improvement of the whole can you hope that your own moral and material conditions will improve. Generally speaking, you cannot, even if you would, separate your life from that of humanity; you live in it, by it, for it. Ask yourself then whenever you do an action in the sphere of your country, or your family: if what I am doing were done by all and for all, would it advantage or injure humanity? And if your conscience answers, it would injure humanity, desist, even if it seem to you that an immediate advantage for your country or your family would ensue from your action. Be apostles of this faith, apostles of the brotherhood of nations, and of the unity of the human race—a principle admitted today in theory, but denied in practice. Be such apostles wherever and in whatever way you are able."

It is rare, indeed, that a priest of the Catholic Church can quote with enthusiastic endorsement the doctrines of Italy's nineteenth-century Jacobins, and if it is possible on this point to do so it is only because here the revolutionary speaks a doctrine which, like so many others, the world owes to traditional religion.

However, the broad "blue print" that has evolved out of the original *beata pacis visio* remains a chimera, another *douce chimere, unless* and *until* there is fully operative among us the moral ingredient that serves as the catalyst that brings the vision from the speculative and intellectual order to work in the practical order of accomplishment. I suggest that this catalytic moral ingredient is, quite simply, the *Will for Peace*.

In this connection, some fairly simple, straightforward talk is urgently in order. It is not certain that a genuine *Will for Peace* exists in our communities or in any notable part of them. It may be true—it probably is—that there is among us an imprecise, diffuse desire for peace, a "hankering" after peace, a preference for peace, any number of other wistful longings in the direction of peace—as there might be in the direction of other moral values or virtues. But most of these do not constitute the *Will for Peace* nor even a substantial stage toward it.

Perhaps my point is best made by appeal to one of the distinctions traditional among the scholastics of my own general philosophical heritage. It has become fashionable to dismiss airily, as devoid of significant content of a solidly philosophical kind, the neat distinctions of the *lexicon peripateticum*. Those of us who set store by them never supposed that they constituted the sum of wisdom nor contained the total treasure of truth; we saw and see them as pegs on which to hang propositions, arguments, points of view, in order to let these be drained of their mere water and tested for their ultimate significance and solid content; we sometimes fear that clarity, the good society and human worth and wisdom themselves have been the casualties of the airy dismissal of the handy little logical pegs and notional distinctions of the dusty, discredited scholastics.

But whatever of all this, one important distinction of schlastic psychology that carries over heavily into scholastic moral philosophy is particularly relevant to the question of an effective *Will for Peace*. I refer to the distinction between *velleitas* and *voluntas*. I submit that though there is a widespread and sometimes warm *velleitas* for peace, there is not so much evidence of that positive and determined *voluntas* in which alone an efficacious *Will for Peace* is at work. I seriously question the motivation, the depth, the sincerity and therefore the work of such *Will for Peace* as may exist among us. I suspect that it is more *velleitas* and short on effective *voluntas*.

Velleitas is to *voluntas* as wishful thinking is to solidly thought—through determined plan; *velleitas* is what moved the youthful Augustine, admiring from afar the beauty of chastity, to pray "Lord, make me chaste—but not too soon!" *Velleitas* means the sneaky regard for a virtue what has no real intention or plan of mastering. *Velleitas* is a desire qualified by all manner of "ifs," "ands" and "buts" that one has no serious disposition to eliminate; *Voluntas* is fixed, stable, unqualified, total commitment; it may fail, but not by my fault, certainly not by my lack of desire, intention and effort to win.

Is our *Will for Peace velleitas or voluntas?* Candor compels the answer. In our national policy (certainly as expressed by secretaries of defense, though in their case more pardonably than in any other) the Will for Security is more urgent, more clear, more unqualified than the Will for Peace, though the latter, in a contingent way, is presumably also present; probably this is not only understandable but, in their case, desirable. But what of our preaching? What of our prayers? Our editorializing? What, even, of our poetry? It is so qualified and so conditioned, so hedged are our bets, that these reveal only the wistfulness, the sentimental desire, the absence of urgency, conviction and controlling purpose which characterizes *velleitas* not *voluntas*. They breathe, no doubt, a love for peace—as the drunkard might cherish an abstract love for sobriety or lecherers a wistful hope of eventual integrity—but they do not add up to the voluntas essential to the *Will for Peace* without which the prospects for peace remain a *douce chimere,* a will-o'-whip, a fantasy never likely to become a fact.

It is the urgent business of religion, on this level and on this front, to create the *Will for Peace* to fortify the *voluntas* of persons and communities to the end that a moral and spiritual climate is created within which positive programs for peace can prosper, without which these, whatever their technical excellence or political skill, must inevitably smother.

Yet even at the point an embarrassment confronts the world of religion. On this, as on so many moral points, our creative efforts of religion are bedevilled by the fact that while we share common objectives and desires, we seek them as a people with a mere *velleitas* if only because in the moral order, is the *desire*. We lack an agreed moral premise from which to proceed, a commonly accepted *moral imperative* to which to appeal or by which to be spurred in a determined common quest for the admittedly common wish for peace. There is not only scant *voluntas* (as opposed to mere *velleitas*) behind our *Will for Peace*); there is *little* religious consensus concerning the roots or the norms of moral responsibility or the motives for moral action. This absence, I repeat, embarrasses us on every moral problem, personal and social; it is especially apparent and unfortunate with respect to peace.

Let us, again, be quite simple and straightforward about this matter of our lack of a commonly accepted moral imperative, even sufficiently common to motivate a *voluntas* for peace. For some of us an ethical imperative which is scarcely more than enlightened self-interest is about *all* we have by way of motivation. For some the voice of reason may be all that speaks to us; for others reason may be a supporting or seconding voice to other sources of moral imperative, sources bound up with a higher order of illumination, of grace or of sanctions. For some the voice of relevation, as fortified by the imperatives or natural law or reason, is all there is, while for others natural law is repudiated entirely and only the imperative of the Gospel is heeded.

In a January (1970) issue of *The Episcopalian* Doctor Nathan Pusey, of Harvard, writes movingly: "The world has never wished to be bothered with the Gospel, and it does not wish to now. Yet it is our conviction that it is precisely in this hostility, or at least indifference, to the Lord—not in rampany population or under-development or threat of war—that the world's most basic need is to be found—always and now."

Certainly I, as a Catholic Christian, could not agree with Doctor Pusey more than I do. But even in what he says, to my mind so accurately—we do not have a moral imperative which speaks univocally and with anything like equal cogency even to all the religious spokesmen gathered in this small room. I do not say this with rue, or reproach, or defeatism; I say it simply with the Christian candor and simplicity needed to put into accurate context for discussion the basic and most embarrassing problem which confronts us in these three days of deliberation about religion and peace. We have no agreed imperative capable of eliciting the needed *voluntas* which gives drive to the *Will for Peace* essential to the realization of world order.

Or have we? Perhaps, at least in this crucial question of

peace, we do have such a commonly accepted imperative, even though it be inoperative, alas, on any other current moral question. I suggest one, though I do so with a certain diffidence.

It has become unfashionable to talk of crusades. Indeed, the mood of the moment is to affect lofty disdain of the very word and to pretend that we have passed beyond the need for crusades, having evolved or matured to a moral level quite superior to the mentality and the methods of the crusade; mayhap, forsooth!

And yet, as one contemplates at once our desperate need for the *Will for Peace* and our lack of cogent, shared imperative evoking such a Will; as one reflects, that is, on the disturbing absence of a moral premise sufficiently widely accepted to be sufficiently effective to provide a common rallying point for the religious contribution to the creation of a climate for peace—then he remembers the word *crusade*. That word now comes back not to haunt one but to give one hope, and with it comes back the premise that yielded the imperative that rallied the crusaders of old: *Dieu le veut!* Perhaps this is the only battle cry to rally the forces for peace to which we are all, as religious people, likely to be respondent:

Perhaps all our separate and therefore, in the social order, ineffective moral imperatives can be synthesized in this, at least so far as the peace of mankind is concerned: *God wills it! Dieu le veut.*

If we cannot agree on that premise, as men and women aware of God and responsive to Him, then God only knows on what we can agree. But if we can and do agree that God wills our peace and demands that we will it, then we are well on the way to that "war on war" which Pius XII asked twenty years ago that all men unite in declaring—a war on war the Pope saw as morally required by the recently finished (1944) "picture of Hell, against which anyone who cherishes a sense of humanity desires more than anything else to close the door forever" (Piu XII, Christmas message 1944).

141

XI

The Cult of Mary in the Age of the Cult of the Flesh

Our Catholic faith and our consequent Catholic moral, ascetical and spiritual teaching are replete, heavily influenced by the purity, the angelic virtue, the chaste spirituality of Mary. But the culture all around us, the civilization which we share with our generation, is once again filled with emphasis on the flesh and especially on the satisfaction, sometimes not only licentious but also violent, of the demands of the flesh. In its commercial advertising, its entertainment, its everyday living, our culture tends to exploit, to exaggerate and to satiate the instincts of flesh.

Hence the need for a renewed theology concerning Mary "our tainted nature's solitary boast," as the protestant poet called her, the living personification of the highest ideals of chastity. Hence the need for a Christian "theology concerning the flesh," so that our culture may be refined by it, our civilization may be cured of excess and purified of decadence, our lives made *sane* and *holy* by it. For the flesh must also be made sacred; human nature must never become mere flesh, least of all de-spiritualized, animal flesh.

This is one of the master problems of our times; it has always been a grave problem for believers in the spirit who none-the-less must live by the flesh, for creatures of flesh who are called to live by the spirit, for humanity born of Adam and Eve but reborn by the grace of Jesus brought to us thanks to Mary, the Madonna of Pompei, is a symbol, a key ot the answer.

Under her title of the *Madonna di Pompei,* the Virgin Mother of Christ and of all the redeemed most especially *symbolizes* and *solves* the problem of a "theology of flesh." The word flesh has suggestive overtones that strike a discordant note in the Marian theme that runs through our Catholic litany: *Mary most pure, Mary most chaste, Mary inviolate.*

In an earlier age, the word had similar overtones and even more diabolical undertones. But it was precisely to free the word of such evil connotations that St. John, in the prologue to his Gospel, chose the word *flesh* and no other to announce the mystery of the Incarnation wherein the "Word became Flesh." It was precisely to underscore the sanctity of the flesh that the earliest Christian creed closed with a profession of faith in the resurrection of the flesh. Today, there is an urgent need to reassert the sanctity of the flesh to free the very word from the morbid or half-evil connotation that surrounds it, to inspire the word with the reverence that it deserves. To this purpose we have decided to speak today of *Mary* and the *flesh* to suggest the relation of the cult of Mary and the great Marian dogmas to what may be called the "theology of the flesh."

When we think of Mary's influence on the theology of the early Church, we usually begin with the Council of Ephesus, held in the year 431. Here, the divinity of Christ was upheld against Nestorius by an appeal to Mary's most privileged title. Theotókos, Mother of God. And yet Mary's influence in controlling Christian teaching goes back to the very infancy of the Church, to those early years when the question "What think ye of Christ?" was first put to the pagan.

It is in these early decades that we find a group called Docetists on the fringe of the Christian community which denied not so much the divinity of Christ as His humanity. Their name came from the Greek word *dokein,* to appear, to seem, to make-believe. These earliest of heretics taught that Christ's body was but a phantom, that He only seemed to be born of a woman, that His suffering, death and resurrection were only make-believe. Strangely enough, the Docetists found it more credible that Christ should be in some sense a Son of God than that He should be the Son of Mary. *

In the letters to the Christians at Ephesus and at Smyrna, St. Ignatius reveals the basic problem that confronted the Docetists. It is the *scandal of the flesh.* That the word should take flesh from a woman, that the Eucharist should perpetuate on earth the mystery of the word enfleshed, that the flesh should be capable of the gift of immortality, such an exaltation or apotheosis of flesh was blasphemous to these proto-heretics. Christians, writes Ignatius to the Ephesians, "must beware of them, for they are hard to cure." There is only one physician, both carnal and spiritual, born and unborn, God become man, true life in death, sprung both from Mary and from God, first subject to suffering and then incapable of it—Jesus Christ Our Lord." And to the Smyrnaeans he writes: "From Eucharist and prayer they hold aloof, because they do not confess that the Eucharist is the flesh of our Saviour, Jesus Christ, which suffered for our sins, and which the Father in His loving kindness raised from the dead."

To the pagan the great stumbling block to an acceptance of Christianity was the *scandalum crucis, the scandal of the cross.* To the Docetist Christians the great stone of stumbling was the *scandalum carnis, the scandal of the flesh.* That the Christian God was born of a woman's flesh was unthinkable. To the pagan and the Jew the great obstacle was the tomb. To the Docetist it was even more the womb. No wonder that the Church in her great hymn of prase, *Te Deum Laudamus,* addresses Christ: "Tu ad liberandum suscepturus hominen, non horruisti Virginis uterum— Thou, when about to take man's deliverance, didst not draw back in horror of the Virgin's womb."

This abhorrence of the flesh which runs through Docetist

---

*It will be clear that this historical section is in great part a summary of the much more scholarly paper of Father Paul Palmer, S.J., Mary and the Flesh, in the collection Mary and Modern Man (America Press 1954).

teaching was not something native to classical paganism. On the contrary, pagan mythology made indulgent sport of the carnal amours of its gods with mortals, as for example, precisely at Pompei. The attitude underlying Docetism was of eastern origin. Some five centuries before the Christian era, on the far eastern borders of Persia or Iran, Zoroaster had spoken of the irreconcilable conflict between Light and Darkness, Spirit and Matter, Good and Evil.

In even more remote India, the Buddha Gautama had proclaimed his antagonism against the material universe and taught that peace could result only with its annihilation.

Just when this alien pessimism entered the Graeco-Roman world, it is difficult to say, but it was already present when Christianity was first being preached, and it was destined to grow with Christianity as an ugly and sometimes infectious influence on Christians. How serious this rival philosophy or religion was is proved by the attention that the earliest Christian writers gave it. It is they who first gave it a name and it is principally from them that we learn of is strange and even fantastic doctrines.

Gnosticism was the name given to this heresy. It had no necessary stigma, being derived from the Greek word *gnosis* which simply means knowledge but not that Christian knowledge which is based on faith and which leads to charity. It was a speculative knowledge, a knowledge which "puffeth up" with pride and a knowledge devoid of charity; it was cold intellectualism.

This element of pride is seen in the idea of one religion designed for the intellectuals, and another for the ignorant masses. For the Christian wisdom founded on faith was God's free gift to the simple and to the wise alike, to the unlettered as well as the lettered, to the weak even more than to the strong. For the Gnostic, wisdom was the fruit of man's own reasoning and could be possessed only by the *elite,* by men of intellect and refinement. Salvation by way of faith, informed by charity, was the goal set for the Christian; salvation by way of knowledge, *gnosis,* was the goal set for the Gnostic. The Gnostic's "vocation was not to believe but to know."

All the Gnostics are not yet dead. They publish articles regularly and have "renewed" their theology for our generation and our age in the life of the Church. They frequently peddle their élitism in expensive lectures and learned journals alleged to contain the doctrine of the "new" Church.

Their basic dualism between faith and experience, between matter and spirit, between the soul and the flesh, which is common to almost every form of Gnosticism, had quite opposite results in the sphere of practical morality. In some, it manifested itself in an exaggerated asceticism which endeavored to mortify the flesh, to kill the flesh, in order to set the soul free of its imprisoning influence.

There has been a tendency among writers who do not fully understand Christian faith and spirituality to identify the asceticism of these extremists with the genuine Christian attitude towards marriage and the other good things of God's creation. Even when there is a surface similarity, the motives that prompted Gnostics and Christians to forego marriage, meat, wine and property are wholly different. "The Church praises renunciation," writes Epiphanius "but she does not condemn marriage; she preaches poverty, but does not inveigh intollerably against those who possess property . . . many in the Church abstain from certain kinds of food, but do not look with contempt upon those who do not so abstain" (Panarion).

Admittedly there were some Christians, clergy as well as laymen, who were prompted to a life of renunciation from motives more Gnostic than Christian. But the attitude of the Church towards such is revealed in the following disciplinary decree which dates back to the fourth century: "If a bishop, priest, deacon or any other member of the clergy abstains from marriage, flesh meat and wine from the motive of contempt and not from the motive of ascetism, he is unmindful of the fact that God made all things exceedingly good, that He made man male and female. In His blasphemy He condemns creation; therefore let Him be corrected, or deposed and ejected from the Church; and the same applies to a layman." (CF. The Apostolic Constitution, VIII,c.51 ed by F.X. Funk)

St. Paul was a celibate and he encouraged others to embrace the same kind of life, but he recognized that "each one has his own gifts from God" (1 Corinthians 7, 17). He recognized as well that the renunciation of marriage could be prompted by motives diabolical as well as divine, and it is against an incipient Gnosticism that St. Paul warns Timothy: "Now the spirit expressly says that in after times some will depart from the faith, giving heed to deceitful spirits and doctrines of devils, speaking lies hypocritically, and having their consciences branded. They will forbid marriage, and will enjoin abstinence from food which God has created to be partaken of with thanksgiving by the faithful and by those who know the truth. For every creature of God is good, and nothing is to be rejected that is accepted with thanksgiving. For it is sanctified by the word of God and prayer" (1 Timothy 4, 15).

There is, however, another aspect or phase of Gnostic morality which manifested itself in an unbridled licentiousness, a conscious effort to free oneself of the law of the flesh by flouting it. So long as the soul feasted on the true knowledge or gnosis, it could not be defiled by so worthless a thing as the body or so inconsequestial a thing as carnal sin. Like the more ascetical minded of their confreres, they too would repudiate marriage lest they perpetuate the kingdom of darkness by imprisoning souls in the flesh, but there were other means of gratifying their lusts and there is sufficient evidence in the history of every Gnostic group that they speedily found them.

It is this form of "emancipated" Gnosticism, of moral self-centered permissiveness in matters sexual—and therefore basic to carnal activity and theory—that is insurgent, indeed dominant, in our day, not only in areas of commerce and amusement, but also

147

of ideology, even in some "theologies." Anyone who does not "spot" it clearly has not been reading our "best" articles on sex education and "toward a theology of sexuality for the modern Catholic"—whoever he may be!

I shall not linger on historic perversions of Christian spirituality and consequent forgetting of Catholic truth concerning the dignity of human flesh, nor on the lessons concerning the perfection of Mary by the power of God, especially in what pertains to the relations between spirit and flesh in sound Christian doctrine. Suffice it to recall the errors of the Manicheans, against whom St. Augustine waged intellectual battle; the excesses of the Albigensians, with their perverse theories of "perfection" and of Christian "fulfillment"; against these latter St. Dominic preached specifically a fervent Catholic cult of Mary to emphasize at once the true primacy of the spirit and the dignity as well as beauty of the flesh.

This cult of Mary took the popular form, encouraged by St. Dominic, of the beloved rosary, with its constant repetition of the *Ave Maria*:—the salute of the angel of God to flesh full of grace, to flesh within fallen humanity, to a womb blessed by its fruit, the Son conceived by the Holy Spirit to become "true God of true God" who became *flesh* for us, for us who are flesh, and for our salvation, being born of the *flesh* of the Virgin Mary of the Immaculate Conception, "theology of the flesh."

I pass over the denial of the doctrine concerning Mary by many of the Protestant theologies of centuries gone by, and I merely mention the concomitant disdain of the flesh, which even extended to the sacred flesh of Christ, which, in fact, was one of the characteristics of many Protestant theological aberrations, as well as later Catholic deviations from faith and order.

Such forgetfulness of the humanity of Jesus and denial of the dignity of the flesh of Mary, somehow shared by every redeemed Christian, made felt its pessimistic influence among Protestant Puritans and Catholic Jansenists. It led many to reject everything but the spirit—and that spirit badly understood—even to the point

148

of condemning flesh as evil, the Church as mere institution, liturgy as sensual, oral prayer itself and the sacramental life as "concessions" to the flesh. Inevitably, such fury and nonsense led to reactions of libertinism—as Puritanism always does—and to a false cult of the flesh, undisciplined by revolt against order rather than enjoyed in the freedom that comes from truth.

So today one who watches with solicitude both the things of God and the things of man, the needs of the spirit and the needs of the flesh, sees the return to these related but seemingly opposite heresies, the names of which our generation forgets but the ideas of which are still at work in our minds and hearts. Gnosticism and Manicheism are still alive, aggressive, unrestrained. Sometimes they are offered as a "new morality"—though they are centuries old, as old as the oldest temptations of our race, temptations both to presumption and to despair, to pride of flesh and to the torment of self-contempt.

But the Church still speaks with sanity of the supremacy, the dignity, the beauty of the flesh when it conforms to the plan, the loving law of its Creator and the grace of its Redeemer.

Undoubtedly, the Spirit of God "bloweth where he wills," and He comes to us not only through the spirits of men but also through the medium of the flesh and through the fleshly symbols which are the material of our daily lives as well as the instruments of His Body—note well the word—which is the organized, institutional Church—the Church of the Incarnate Word.

Specifically, on the level of human love made divine by a special sacrament, Matrimony, under the guidance of our Holy Father, Pope Paul and the teaching of the Vatican Council concerning the true nature, dignity and sanctity of nuptial love, there is a growing awareness among Catholics that love must not be divorced from the primary purpose of marriage, which is the child, that love is really fruitful in the child, that the marriage debt must be regarded as an expression of love, not merely a demand of justice. Experience has proved that where the primary and secondary values of marriage are separated, there is danger that a man will take a wife for child bearing and a mistress for love-making, or, what has actually come to pass in much of our own society as a result of improved methods of birth-prevention and easy divorce, turn his wife into a mistress until her ability to satisfy his lust wanes. Theologians of an earlier day were correct in ensuring a love that sought expression in lust; for lust is a promiscuous tendency that must destroy love.

As we celebrate the feast of the Immaculate Conception, we must be reminded time and again of Mary's most privileged titles if we are to develop a holy and healthy "theology of the flesh" as well as a sound cult of Mary. But there is one title that we must not forget, a title first given to her by St. Cyril of Alexandria in a panegyric delivered years ago: "Hail, from us, Mary, Mother of God. . . . Sceptre of Orthodoxy." Next to her Son, Mary, more than any other, has contributed most to that necessary sanity, marked with reverence, that must characterize any true theology of the flesh. For in Her and through Her has flesh been glorified and sanctified, reaching its apotheosis in the Resurrection of Her Son and in Her own glorious Assumption, according to the flesh.

If it be true—thus far, God knows, it remains to be proved—that underneath the modern neo-pagan cult of the flesh, there is the beginning of a new and sane humanism recognizing the dignity of the flesh and the full and true dignity of human nature, then, if this be true, there is needed more than ever a cult of Mary and of all the virtues of which the Virgin is at once the symbol, the realization by the power of God, and the example to us, her brothers and sisters.

There is needed more than ever a certain clear, powerful persuasive witness, so long traditional in Christian spirituality. Sometimes it was made weak by neglect, by imperfect motives, by half-hearted practice, by obscure or negative understanding. But it produced not only Saints, but also civilization. It was the ancient Christian witness to such virtues and practices as chastity, virginity, celibacy, renunciation for the sake of the kingdom, even to the desire ot be like the angels themselves.

It is necessary to remember these witnesses always—not only on the feast of the Immacolata—and it is opportune to proclaim that need here in the Basilica of the Madonna that makes holy the land of Pompei, of Herculaneum, the land of ancient pagan memories expelled by the faith and virtue of our Saints—above all Maria Santissima!

Thus by the teachings of the feast of the Madonna the old instincts of Pompei are dominated, the flesh is made the twin of the Spirit—no longer its rival, but one with the spirit in love and service. Thus we become what Man was when he walked in the garden, Master of himself, steward (guardian) of all creation, the Friend of God. Thus we become, each day in some degree, what some day we shall be when the Church has done her work and Christ shall come again to decide who will live forever with the Madonna and with God Himself—and who must perish—even as did Sodom and Gomorrah—or ancient Pompei.

XII

The Roman Loyalty
of the English Martyrs

Every devout Catholic, I dare say everyone who claims the name of Christian or who senses the dignity of what it is to be a conscientious person of whatever integral commitment, rejoices in the news from Rome of the canonization of the forty English and Welsh martyrs.

There are inevitable shadings in the reasons for rejoicing with respect to canonizations. Such is the case when a mere girl is canonized, like Maria Goretti. Such is the case in the canonization of saints from the Third World, from nations or tribes which, in our limited vision, we sometimes see as beyond the frontiers of what, for cultural rather than theological reasons, we have tended to think of as the Christian world. Such is the case when a great social worker is canonized, or a saint who happens to be a surpassing scholar (or *vice versa*), or a witness to a special virtue seemingly more relevant and more "popular" in centuries gone by and lands afar.

So, too, in the case of the forty English and Welsh martyrs. The reasons for rejoicing in their canonization are nuanced and not without differences. There are not a few who rejoice that the Holy See, without compromising its ecumenical aspirations and proper spirit of openness to new hopes and directions among all Christians, has acted with what appears to them to be a certain boldness, not to say defiance of the mood of the hour, in proclaiming the special excellence of these men and women who dared to be different, refusing to conform with the demands of the hour and the expectations of what turned out to be the "majority."

There is, in fact, small reason for special rejoicing under this heading. If the Holy See were to be forgetful of those who bore such historic witness to that See and to all the premises on which it rests, she would be forgetful of the very promises of Christ by which she is sustained and her special mission to proclaim and to praise fidelity to those promises in order to raise up new future good servants of the King or the community, to be sure, but of Christ and His Kingdom first.

Others rejoice in the canonization because they see in it, very properly, a salute by the Universal Church to the lonely place of a right conscience in the midst of the tumult of disputations and the chaos of changing times, cultures and moral codes. Many—I confess to be among these—rejoice in the simultaneous canonization of a litany of martyrs which includes laymen and clergy, men and women, priests diocesan and religious, aristocrats and simple folk, in a word, a cross-section of representatives of all who constitute the strength and the variety of a land that speaks our English tongue.

Some, more narrowly, may take particular delight precisely in the fact that these saints are English, "some of our own, at last!". I was in St. Peter's when Thomas More and John Fisher were canonized these many years ago and I shall never forget the mingled sentiments of amusement and yet holy joy with which I heard a good woman from Liverpool, all of us lost in the mob far nearer the obelisk of St. Peter's Square than the altar of St. Peter's Basilica, reply to her husband when he announced from his perilous vantage point on the base of a column that the Pope had just read the bull declaring the canonization of More and Fisher: "Thank God there are now saints in heaven who understand English!". I seconded the motion, but reflected that it was what they *said* in English, rather than their facility in the tongue, that won for them the honors of the altar.

Our Holy Father, Pope Paul, has given his own reasons for

153

rejoicing in an address to the College of Cardinals May 18, 1970. He speaks of his "great joy" and "own wish" as he reports the unanimous petition of the Consistory to salute as saints the martyrs of England and Wales whose canonization he then fixed for October 25. He then sets forth the special reasons for his joy and his wish, as well as for the "highly appropriate" timing of the canonization. He sees in their recognition "a most effective way of promoting the good of the Church, at a time when she is making every endeavor to bring back unity to all Christians, and to maintain and strengthen those common human and Christian values whose existence is being threatened by the encroachments of materialism."

He reveals that he is not unmindful of the argument that these martyrs died in times of a confusion and a spirit perhaps different to those in our own day and he repudiates any intention of opening up old wounds or adding to the bewilderment of our times by recalling controversies now dormant, at least, and even, please God, dead. Nonetheless, putting fully aside the rancors of the past and its memories of sorrow, the Holy Father insists that the present canonizations are filled with lessons for the future:

"First of all, they are a shining example of that genuine faith, which will have nothing to do with ambiguity or false compromise in whatever is held as sacred: a faith that is never afraid to declare its convictions. Such a faith is a necessary condition of all true and fruitful ecumenical dialogue.

"At the same time, these Martyrs are especially noteworthy as examples of true Christian charity towards those who do not profess the same Christian faith. In an age when religious controversy stirred up so much hatred, it is most heart-warming to notice that such attitudes are completely foreign to these heroes of the Christian faith. Rather the reverse, as the acts of their martyrdom witness: many of them showed themselves as only too ready to surrender their lives with the greatest willingness for the spiritual welfare of their fellow countrymen.

"Finally, we cannot pass over in silence the fact that this canonization is most opportune for another reason, and it is this. Today, materialistic and naturalistic philosophies of life are gaining ground and are threatening to deprive us of the spiritual heritage of our civilization. These blessed Martyrs, who did not hesitate to sacrifice their very lives in obedience to the clear voice of conscience and the will of God, are a glowing testimony to human dignity and liberty. And their witness is all the more precious since it comes from a group of men and women representing so many different walks of life."

Considerations, perhaps, of personal delicacy and official reserve may have suggested to the Holy Father that he abstain from explicit exposition of the substance, content and precise point of the "precious witness" to which these so many and different English and Welsh martyrs gave their love, their example and their lives. That witness was to the claims of the Holy Father himself, the special Primacy of Peter and His Successors, the unique place in the Universal Church of the Apostolic See of Rome. Unless this be clear in all considerations of the case, the story is without point and the witness unto martyrdom is in vain. The forty martyrs whose memory rejoices us in these occasionally melancholy times are witnesses to the *Romanità,* properly understood and never to be downgraded, of authentic Catholicism in England. That *Romanità* dates from England's own Augustine. It is proclaimed in the patronage of so many of her Cathedrals, monasteries, religious institutions. Its presence, often forgotten but never destroyed, abides in some of England's proudest traditions and happiest phrases: Defender of the Faith is only one.

There are, therefore, those of us who particularly rejoice in the present canonizations because they reaffirm, dramatically and unforgettably, the ties with Rome and with the Bishop of Rome which have never ceased to characterize, with a fervor rarely found elsewhere, the Catholicism of England. Those ties are not political nor, except in certain humanistic elements, merely cultural. They do not reveal themselves only in exuberant proclamations *From the Flaminian Gate* or in prophetic hopes of a *Second Spring* of Catholicism in England, dismissed by the unthinking as romantic, poetic gestures. They are not inconsistent with any of the essential elements of the native English genius; quite the contrary. They are summed up in the word *Romanità*, not as it is mocked in contemporary cocktail discussions of theology, but as it was profoundly operative in the witness of the English martyrs and remains operative in English Catholicism's loyalty to the Roman Magisterium as well as it own traditions of Catholic faith.

I venture to add a further perhaps official but also, I feel, deeply personal reason for rejoicing in these canonizations. That reason derives from the nature of the post it is my privilege to hold as Prefect for the Congregation for the Clergy and from the fact that I am a priest. The priests in the list of the newly canonized martyrs are, like Thomas More, men for all seasons. They are, unmistakably, men for our own times. In the midst of the grimness and lack-luster standardization of our society in so many of its aspects, they strike a note of joy, urbanity, humanism, hope, unconquerable faith and conquering love. They represent the English priesthood at its best, which, for me, has meant, since first I came to know English priests over thirty years ago, the Catholic priesthood in its finest expression. In this alone I find ample reason for rejoicing in the recent Roman ceremonies.

One of the martyrs, Edmund Campion, anticipated the grounds of my rejoicing when he said: "There will never want in England men that will have care of their own salvation, nor such as shall advance other men's. Neither shall this Church here ever fail, so long as priests and pastors shall be found for their sheep, rage man or devil never so much."

Another, Ralph Sherwin of the Venerable English College in Rome, reflected the spirit which rejoices me when, with typical British understatement and wry humor, he described the clanking of the chains which throughout his captivity bound his feet: "I wear now on my feet and legs some little bells to keep me in mind who I am, and Whose I am. I never heard such sweet harmony before."

But no one proclaimed more proudly what the priests of the British Isles thought of themselves, their dignity, their special vocation and their relationship both to time and to eternity (I speak of the days before sacerdotal "identity crises") than did the Welshman David Lewis. No mere doctrinnaire theologian or priest by social position and Catholic by family inheritance, he was known as *Tady Tlodion* (Father of the Poor). Let his words, uttered in the moment of his martyrdom, sum up the special reasons for priestly rejoicing which move my heart as I pen these lines:

"Here is a numerous assembly—may the great Saviour of the world save every soul of you all. I believe you are here met not only to see a fellow-native die, but also to hear a dying fellow-native speak. My religion is the Roman Catholic; in it I have lived above these forty years; in it I now die, and so fixedly die, that if all the good things in this world were offered me to renounce it, all should not remove me one hair's breadth from my Roman Catholic faith. A Roman Catholic I am; a Roman Catholic priest I am; a Roman Catholic priest of that religious order called the Society of Jesus I am; and I bless God who first called me. I was condemned for reading Mass, hearing confessions, and administering the sacraments. As for reading the Mass, it was the old, and still is the accustomed and laudable liturgy of the holy Church; and all the other acts are acts of religion tending to the worship of God, and therefore dying for this I die for religion."

God grant us myriad priests of equal clarity and courage in these days of convenient compromise with conscience and a certain desire not to be too "Roman."

XIII

Toast to the Holy Father

Contrary to the caricature drawn by those who like to describe the Church as a "static" institutional organization, at least until their own arrival on the scene, the Holy Catholic Church is always in the process of beginning again. Such is the case within each of us singly; as Julian Greene remarked years ago, it is necessary to be reconverted to Catholicism every morning in order to remain faithful to our earliest ideals. Such it is in the history of the Church herself; she is always in the process of beginning again.

Historical fact confirms this, even if theology did not proclaim it on the level of theory. Her temporal goods are repeatedly confiscated by enemies from without; her buildings are closed, her properties decay or are squandered, dissipated, allowed to run to ruin by the inept or the misguided within. Some of her sons and daughters in every generation abandon her, some of them to turn on her with fury; others remain within her community, in more or less formal fashion, and tear her apart from their vantage point from among the visible fold. When large numbers leave, their departure is frequently described (whether it be that of nations or notable individuals) as a tragic blood-letting or a brain drain, even when, on occasion, in purely human terms, it is more like the lancing of an abscess.

In any case the Church is always beginning again, building anew, both in her historical presence in the world and in the interior life of her very soul, the presence of the Spirit within her. In the visible realm of this world she is always building in new styles to meet new tastes, new places of worship where old styles have become obsolete; new centers for education and human refinement, adapting new curricula and new trends to her perennial witness. She is continually organizing new programs of service which seek to blend her divine witness with new human cultures. Her mission, in every place and time, remains constant: it is that which in a century of savagery not so very different from our own, once surface and secondary features are stripped away, Paulinus of Nola described to a new bishop of the Church in these terms:

" . . . *per te barbari discunt*
resonare Christum corde Romano
placidamque vitam vivere casti."

In our own day those structures and works of the Church which share in the evolution of our society give signs of being obsolete, unworkable. The Church does not, on that account, bog down or abandon the world. She seeks rather an *aggiornamento* in which new structures, better adapted to the difficulties and opportunities of the day, may be put to work toward the ancient, unchanging and perennial purposes of achieving human sanity and divine salvation.

The Church, which is promised eternity and, although she be merely the initial phase of the Kingdom of God, partakes of God's own permanence, never supposes in the work of her apostolate that she has accomplished perfecton or established an absolute historical victory over the forces of disintegration within or without her earthly presence. She is always seeking to perfect her means of spiritual service, using her art of blending, in proper and effective proportions, the old and the new: the traditions to which she is bound by faith and the progress to which she is called by her nature. As at the time of the impetus which Christ gave to her direction toward the coming of the Kingdom, so time and again in history, and never more clearly than now, at the height of the discouragement of seeming to have accomplished nothing after many labors, she throws down her nets again at the command of Christ and in accord with the obedient word of Peter.

Note carefully the content of the command from the lips of

Christ to which I allude. Note also the nature and significance of the response of Peter. Christ, as once on the lake of Palestine, perpetually renews His command to the Church: "Seek further depths!" *Duc in altum!* And Peter, first speaking for himself the mind of all his company, then later speaking through Leo the Great, Gregory the Great, Leo XIII, Pius XI, Pius XII, John XXIII and now Pope Paul, invariably replies, for himself and for us all: "Lord, we have labored all night and have taken nothing. Nevertheless—even though it seems a moment that gives scant prospect for success, at Thy Word—*in verbo tuo*—we shall let down the nets and begin again!"

Observe carefully at Whose Word the net is lowered. Recall accurately the circumstances which make the command, humanly speaking, unlikely of success. Reflect upon the unhesitating, obedient response of Peter and the prompt cooperation of those who surround him. And then remember the bountiful catch that followed on the first, as it has on subsequent responses of Peter to Christ and of the company of believers to Peter. All this is a lesson for the times.

Let me be more pointed. Call to mind the incident related in the sixth chapter of St. John's Gospel. There Christ is threatened with perhaps the first of what has come to be called the "brain drains" from the body of His followers. The point at issue, oddly enough, is the question of His Real Presence in the Eucharist. Many of those in His company (the first members of His historic Church according to the New Law) have begun to murmur. Their reasons are not indicated and therefore one may not call into question their intellectual integrity or considerations of their subjective conscience. We are only told that they *quit,* leaving behind them the explanation that they found the Word of the Lord "a hard saying," something that surpassed their capacity for faith and order. Again, note well who speaks up for the "college" of the twelve in order to say what His Successor, specifically at this moment in the history of the Church, says for us all on this same point of faith. It is Peter and his response is ours: "Lord, to whom else shall we go? Thou alone hast the words of eternal life."

Sometimes it is said that, with the passing centuries, the ancient and holy simplicities of the Christian community have become overladen, even smothered, under the accretions of multiple cultures and the assertion of the human, the historical and the temporal, includng the political. As a result, we are frequently invited to strip away antique Roman anad other pagan accumulations, "medieval accretions," Renaissance pretenses, counter-Reformation defensive influences or attitudes. It might also be in order to strip away some of the later vocabulary and theorizing which have also helped to obscure the primitive clarity of the total Christian experience by veiling it in more recent conceits and more contemporary philosophical, political and cultural fashions.

And so, suppose we forget for a half-hour or so the disputations of the Church Fathers, the Constantinian donations, the collapse and the heritage of the empires of the East and the West, the speculations and also the superstitions of the Middle Ages, the bombast of the Reformation and the rise of nationalism, the subtleties of scholasticism and the confines, if you will, of Canon Law; suppose we suspend for a moment debates about nature and grace, Transubstantiation, sacramental symbolism, feudal ceremonial and democratic opinion polling. Let us seek no less a relief from exploration into the mysteries of existentialism, the flotsam and jetsam of phenomenology, the moodiness of modernism and the excitement of the new sciences. Let us close our eyes momentarily to all the historic structures, classical and contemporary alike, and our minds to all the intellectual developments since the beginning, developments theological, philosophical and cultural—in order that we may focus our attention, clearly and cleanly, on things as they were at the beginning.

If we thus return, in spirit at least, to these beginnings, in order that we may assess all subsequent developments, what do we find? If the New Testament has any worth, we find two men

161

standing face to face by the lakeshore of Galilee. One is Jesus, Son of Mary. The other is Simon, son of John. Simon is a young fisherman and he has a boat. Jesus is known in His community as the son of a carpenter, and He is also young. The accounts left us of the friendship between these two men, their relationships and conversations, their characters and the influence of the One over the other, reveal, little by litle, that the One, Jesus, is the Christ, the Son of the Living God. Even on a lakeshore in an obscure corner of a conquered province of the Roman Empire, the staggering but unmistakable fact is that He understands and proclaims Himself to be the Man of Nazareth, to be sure, but also *God among men,* sent by His Eternal Father to initiate the full teaching of God's Kingdom and to establish a Church which would continue that teaching to the ends of the earth and to the end of time.

The same Scriptural accounts reveal that the other,—his name significanctly changed from Simon to Peter (the Rock),—is destined to be the first to declare in open, unequivocal terms, succinct terms of a type held in scant repute in our more word times, the Divinity, the Lordship, the Authority of this Jesus and to become the first, in time and in eminence, of the living cornerstones of the Church as established by Jesus.

In other words, the simple, primitive, central fact is that One of these young men is the Christ, the only Teacher commissioned by God Himself; the other is to be the Vicar of that Christ in a sense which, however subsequent human speculation, theological included, may attempt to extenuate, dilute or explain it away, remains historically and theologically special to Peter and to His Successor, the Bishop of Rome—whoever that Bishop may be, however many the well-founded claims to be heard of his brothers in the collegiate company of the successors to the eleven associated with him, whatever may be the changing political, cultural or temporal circumstances of human history.

If we thus return to what was at the beginning, we overhear other fragmentary but unforgettable conversations between these two. These conversations are many. I have already alluded to two. If we focus our attention on this scene by the lakeside, we hear a third. It is one of several such conversations which have shaped all subsequent history, sacred and profane, conversations which explain, after these 2,000 years, the fervor with which we here present speak of the Pope and the faith by which we, as our fathers, have been bound to Him, to Peter and to Christ since first we began to breathe the life of Catholic faith.

Let us listen to that lakeshore conversation with special care. It is crucial to the crisis of the Christian community today. Jesus said: "Peter, lovest thou Me more than these others?" And Peter, with threefold protestation, replied: "Lord, Thou knowest all things, Thou knowest that I love Thee." Whereupon he received from the lips of the Son of God Himself the mandate to nourish the Christian community with truth, to feed the followers of Christ with divine strength.

In other conversations between these two, Christ illumined the content and extent of this commission: "But I have prayed for thee, Peter, that thy faith fail not: and thou, being once converted, confirm thy brethren!"

Nor did Peter long delay in demonstrating not only his acceptance but his understanding of that commission. In the Acts of the Apostles we find him already hard at work, conscious of his role as Primate in the Collegiate Church. I shall not plague you with what have come to be called "proof texts" (though they *are* texts of the Sacred Scriptures and they *do* prove the point I am recalling, but need not belabor at a gathering of *Romani*); I mention but a few which have taken on a peculiar and poignant relevance in our particular moment of turbulent history:

"But Peter, standing up with the eleven, lifted up his voice and spoke to them: 'Ye men of Judea, and all that dwell in Jerusalem, be this known to you and with your ears receive my words'" (Acts 2, 14).

" . . . they brought forth the sick into the streets, and laid them

163

on beds and couches, that when Peter came his shadow at the least might overshadow any of them, and they might be delivered from their infirmities" (Acts 5, 15). (God grant us a like healing when the shadow of His Successor passes among us in the pilgrimages he makes to the ends of the earth in quest for peace in the world and within the Church!)

"And when there had been some disputing, Peter, rising up, said to them: 'Men, brethren, you know that in former days God made choice among us that by my mouth the Gentiles should hear the word of the Gospel and believe' " (Acts 15, 7).

Wherein does the challenge of His Successor to the world and to his critics within the Church differ, even today, from these words of Peter? Why should our response be any different in these latter days than was the response of the Collegiate Church to Peter when first he proclaimed this sense of his own "self-identity"? Small wonder that Dr. Eugene Carson Blake, reacting to the murmuring of even some Catholics to words on the lips of Pope Paul at the World Council of Churches ("My name is Peter!"), felt bound to ask: "What else could he call himself, given his claims and his own self-consciousness of his position in the Church?"

In effect, Dr. Blake appears to be reminding us that Paul VI is one priest who suffers from no identity crisis! He knows exactly who he is, for Whom he speaks, what are his theological, spiritual and historical premises. God forbid that he forget them, falling victim to the cultural and religious amnesia that so bewilders contemporary Catholics.

Sometimes the claims of the Primacy, at least as they are presented to us even in some of the writings of our own, strike us as alien, superseded, insensitive to the instincts and needs of our times. Perhaps it is wise on occasion to see our Father's House (the community of faith of which God is the Father, its visible manifestation in the Church of which the Holy Father is the head) from outside the familiar fold in which we sometimes appear to feel more like prisoners than mature sons. For example, what does a representative Mohammedan think of the Pope?

Perhaps Si Hamza Bubakeur, Rector of the Islamic Institute in Paris, speaks the mind of another tradition when, as quoted in *Le Monde,* he thus reacts to Pope Paul: "The teachers of Islam, fully conscious of what Christianity means to the moral equilibrium of individuals and the survival of civilization properly understood, follow with great attention and profound sympathy your (the Pope's) battle against the inevitably transient difficulties of our day. Even as all the followers of the religious traditions which have sprung up in the family of our Patriarch, Abraham, they too hope for the triumph of the spirit over insurgent materialism, of immemorial traditions over dissipating novelties, of eternal dogmas over superficial haphazardness. They admire your courageous and high-minded intransigence born of deep understanding and of sheer determination to lift man to the level of faith, rather than degrade man and faith alike to the level of easy but sterile accommodations. They are convinced that in the midst of the present tempests, the Christian ship is guided by a pilot of lofty and admirable valor. May God come to your aid and reconcile all our friends, the Catholics of the world, even as the Koran would define the case, around the intrepid Vicar that you are, responsible to God and to humanity for the spiritual development of mankind, a development perilously menaced by return to chaos and to a perverted concept of religious life, all in a tormented world!"

Let us be honest about it. Claims so staggering as those of the Pope would be sheer arrogance were they the mere result of a heritage from the collapse of the Roman Empire or the pretensions of Renaissance princes. But you and I remember the Scriptural lakeshore and the conversation of loving mutuality which took place there when this authority and command to service were first communicated from the Son of God Himself. As at that beginning, when Christianity was in the springtime, so now, at this later but still relatively early hour in the life of the Church, at the heart of all the structures, programs, communications, services and panoply there abides that love which was at once the origin and the motive of all else of substance in the history that grew out of the conversations between Jesus and Peter. Peter must still give as the premise of His every claim and service the response given on that day by the lakeshore: "Lord, Thou knowest all things; Thou knowest that I love Thee." Christ still demands that Peter love Him more than he loves all else—public opinion, rivals, friends, critics or self.

I think it not far-fetched to suggest that Jesus, standing in the midst of Catholics today, might develop what He said by the lakeshore, confirming not changing it, by asking for His Vicar, the Successor of Peter, something of what He asked for Himself: "Lovest thou my Vicar more than these others, even having fully in mind their claims, also proclaimed by Me, on your love and your acceptance? Lovest thou Me in Peter more than in these others whose lesser claims are valid but different? Is your love for Me, and for Me even in that Church of which Peter is the living, visible proxy for Me, a premise of the service by which you feed my lambs and feed my sheep—or does your service of others leave Me out and repudiate, if only by ignoring them, the claims of the first law that binds you to love God in Me in order that your love of others, neighbors and enemies alike, may be salutary, firmly-rooted in the love that alone is eternal?"

I have already admitted that these quotations from the lips of Jesus are likely to be dismissed as "proof texts" in our more academic times. I have not had the opportunity to check on their most recent exegesis, though I am aware that Dr. Hans Kung, in his recent book on *The Church,* has indicated, with abundant footnotes and rich *wissenfschaft,* that lines of thought which you and I share concerning the Papacy and the Church as a result of these texts are not, you will be surprised to learn, really bolstered by the rhetoric of a Victorian Protestant historian (Lord Macauley) whom Dr. Kung seems to feel we may have considered a *locus theologicus.* Dr. Kung also points out that Lord Macauley, one regrets to recall, never became a Catholic, a bit of news which I think it is about time to pass on to you.

But on the basis of these texts, and with peace to both the English rhetorician and the German theologian, this only thing I say for the purposes of the toast appropriate to today's gathering of *Romani*: I do know how these words were understood when first we studied them and when love, especially on the lips of a priest, and the Primacy of Peter, especially on the lips of a theologian, had meanings less qualified, less nuanced, less equivocal than these words seem sometimes to have acquired more recently. I know that our answer to the questions I have ventured to put on the lips of Jesus would then have been—as it is now and will forever be—a ringing *Yes*. I also know that we would have been disposed, despite all our sin, ignorance and limitations, to strive at least to fulfill the corollaries of that *Yes* not only in terms of a contemplative love for Christ, a consequent love for His Church and a collaborative love for His Vicar, but also in terms of a lifelong service of His flock, His people, His Kingdom so far as these came within the compass of our love and energy. I feel neither hesitation nor shame in so asserting.

The Primacy of Peter and the place of His Successor in our priestly thought and love did not separate the Papacy from us or us from the Papacy. Quite the contrary; it became a bond among us, a bond stronger than that of blood on occasion, than that of the water of merely human interests always. Karl Adam, a theologian not entirely without *wissenfschaft* and the insights of our generation, once used a beautiful figure of speech to describe how when we Catholic Christians kiss the Fisherman's Ring on the finger of the Pope we embrace one another, wherever in the world we may be, whatever the century in which we live, have lived or may yet live, bound as we are by a single bond of the faith, hope and love which animated the dialogue between Jesus and Peter on the shores of the lake at Galilee.

In the spirit of that love, we strove to learn how a Christian,

167

especially a priest, can love life, the sheer joy of life, without any necessary connection with erotic satisfaction, just so he love for the sake of the Kingdom. He can love learning, beauty, the sick, the poor, his kinsmen, his neighbors, his enemies, the liturgy, music, *the work itself*—but above all, the things of the world to come as well as those of the world around him, so long as he remains faithful to Jesus, to Peter and to the family of God gathered about them, theologically and historically, in the local churches which, through communion with Rome, constitute the Church on earth.

XIV
Pope John and His Secret

On this visit to Genoa you have asked me to talk about Pope John XXIII; and I will do so with great joy, because it seems to me that there is a deep relationship between Pope John's thought and work and the question of vocations.

To be sure, I have not come to look for vocations among you. You are married, and I do not want to upset your marriages! Marriage is a holy state, but it is very different from the priesthood! In the Western world, at least, I suspect that only an ill-informed woman would marry a priest. A priest's work goes on for about 20 hours a day, for about 52 weeks a year, and for the whole of his life. The priestly vocation demands such a complete giving of self that it would be unreasonable and unjust, if not simply crazy, to bind a woman as a wife to the destinies of a Catholic, Apostolic, Roman priest, above all in this twentieth century.

The priest has to be wedded to the Church. He has to be totally dedicated to her. He is a member of every Christian family, the spiritual father of all the children of all families.

If one of you happens to be free to make such a gift of himself . . . good for him . . . ! ! !

But I have to talk to you about Pope John.

Everybody has had somethng to say or has written something about Pope John!

Many have represented him as a sort of revolutionary, especially in the spiritual and above all in the priestly life. But he was nothing of the kind. You only have to read his "Journal of a Soul" to see that he was a priest in the most traditional Catholic pattern. That is to say, his personality, his spirituality and his undertakings

—everything he did and everything he was—derive from a theology of the priesthood and a kind of priestly piety which many of those who make use of his name to justify their own ideas of priestly style of life could not but despise. To tell the truth, they do despise it. The warmth of his personality and his aimiability apart —both obviously consistent with his idea of priestly "style"—he was straight out of the manuals of priestly perfection so common in an age some of us thought (and perhaps hoped) had died with the popularity of the *Imitation of Christ*.

A few examples will be enough to reveal his spirit:

—his attachment to the Spiritual Exercises, every year;

—his devotion to the daily Rosary, and—if I may use the expression—the pastoral quality of his speeches, his desire to be among the people as their leader in prayer, to attend popular feasts and processions;

—his immense veneration for the Holy Fathers of the Church, especially for St. Ignatius of Antioch (the Theophoros - God-bearer) and for all those who fostered orthodoxy in doctrine;

—his love of pastoral teaching for the reform of the social system. We can take the Encyclical *Mater et Magistra* as an example;

—his concern for maintaining the integrity of the Faith of the Fathers, his predecessors, back to the Evangelists and to Jesus himself;

—his motto *Obedientia et Pax*. This did not mean that he was empty-headed and thought that everything was just fine, like someone who cannot see the end of his nose and has no ideas of his own. No, it was the result of an inner struggle which is summed up in the Gospel's words: *abneget semetipsum,* and in St. Ignatius of Antioch's: "It is better to be a Christian and not say so than to say so and not to be so" (Letter to the Ephesians, cap. XV);

—his love for priests, his positive attitude towards ecclesiastical celibacy . . . even to the point of tears! We can say this because we know it from his letters to his family, from one of his spiritual Testaments, from his Encyclicals dealing with other matters, for example, *Pacem in Terris,* and his defence of life and the family . . . not to mention the obligations of his high Magisterium, which he felt profoundly. It may be said, and I am saying it now, that if Pope John had had to write an Encyclical on married love and human life such as Pope Paul VI has had to write, he would certainly have followed the same line of thought, and might have been even stronger;

—his passionate love for children. . . . In regard to this, I think it interesting that the first evening following the solemn opening of the II Ecumenical Council of the Vatican, after speaking to the people who had gathered by torchlight in St. Peter's Square, he bade them good night with the words: "I now give you the blessing. Next to me I love to think that there is the Immaculate Virgin, whose lofty prerogative we are celebrating today (it was October 11th, the liturgical feast of the Divine Motherhood). I have heard that some of you have been recalling Ephesus and the torches that were lit around the basilica in that city on the occasion of the III Ecumenical Council in 431. I saw the remains of Ephesus with my own eyes some years ago, which record the proclamation of the dogmas of Mary's Divine Motherhood. . . . Love of God, love of the brethren. All, buoyed up now by the peace of the Lord, go forward together in good works!

"When you go home you will find your children there. Give them a hug, and say: this is from the Pope. Perhaps you will find some tears needing to be dried. Have a word of comfort for those in pain . . . " (Balducci, *Papa Giovanni,* p. 192). Looking at young people on another occasion, he exclaimed, "So much youthfulness—how can it be concerned only about the things of this earth?" (ib. p. 193).

All this goes to show that if Pope John were a revolutionary, he was one in the way of those who are in the Catholic Church and stay in it, not of those who leave!

In a word, he was no "progressivist." But he was not a

conservative either, nor a reactionary, not even a liberal; he was not a priest of the future, and not even one of the past. He was a priest of that priesthood of Jesus Christ which is of yesterday, today and for ever!

In short: he was loyal to the past, open to the future, and loving toward both. In one word, he was "catholic," in time because he was most devoted to the memories of the past, above all, those of the Faith, but looked forward hopefully to a future more worthy of the human person, of the human family, of the temporal community, and of the Church herself.

This is why some curious characters find it magical that he was so "catholic" in his world-wide appeal despite the fact that he was catholic in space, he was typically Italian, not to say Bergamese. No! He was "Roman," in the broadest and noblest meaning of that word, in the sense that "Christ is Roman," because he shared the needs, sufferings, hopes and yearnings of the whole world: in the Church, from the most aged Cardinal to the youngest Bantu priest; in the human world community, from the highest to the lowest. He shared the interests and labors of Presidents and Prime Ministers as well as those of the most humble workers and peasants.

You may remember photographs of Pope John with President Eisenhower, both of them bursting with laughter, and seen by everyone; you may remember him with a child in a hospital on Christmas morning, both he and the child smiling; with the prisoners in the Regina Coeli jail in Rome, both he and they all smiles; with pilgrims from all over the world—always smiling. What was he smiling at? At the Church? No, no, never! At the world's problems? No, never! Behind those smiles was a heart full of anguish but the patience of God!

That was because he knew that he and others could not solve the Church's problems and the world's problems on their own, but needed help from God, and the merits of the saints, those of the Madonna above all; they needed the wisdom of Tradition, especially of the Faith. The real source of his joy was his joy in the Lord!

He it was who wrote on the occasion of Advent in the first year of his pontificate, to Cardinal Micara, Vicar General of Rome, saying: "Let us be brave, Eminence!". Later on, at Christmas he said in St. Peter's: "Our heart enters your homes, which are all lit up by the warmth of your expectation of the birth of the Divine Saviour; it swells with tenderness, to offer you the greeting of Our fatherly prayers and good wishes. We should like to remain by the tables of the poor, in the workshops, in places of study and science, by the beds of the sick and the old, wherever people pray and suffer and work for themselves and for others! Yes, We should like to lay Our hand on the heads of the little ones, look the young in the eyes, encourage mothers and fathers to do their daily duty! To all We should like to repeat the words of the Angel: I bring you news of great joy: a Saviour is born to you" (E. Balducci, op. cit. p. 194).

From all this we can easily see that Pope John never thought that "God is dead" and that the Church was in a fatal crisis. On the contrary, he believed that the Lord is risen, that the Church is young, that the victory of Christ, of the Church, of the Faith, of Hope and of Charity is all fore-ordained. He took seriously Christ's words: "I have overcome the world. . . . I will be with you even to the end of the world"; and the words of his namesake, the Apostle John: "The victory that overcomes the world: your faith."

He was not revolutionary, certainly not against the Church and her structures, and still less a revolutionary against the faith! What then was the secret of this man in whom all saw, if not the figure of a father, then perhaps that of a grandfather? All felt that about him: Catholics, Orthodox, Protestants, Jews, and atheists.

The secret was simple. He did not love that which we call *humanity,* because humanity of that sort does not exist. It is an abstract thing; it has no face, and no address to which we might send a letter of blame or good wishes, or a Christmas card, or a summons to call at the police station. Humanity has not a trade. Pope John loved *the person, all persons, any person.* Humanity, as such, does nothing good to us or bad to us; it is a concept and cannot be loved or hated by normal people.

Let me take an example. During the same week that I paid my first visit to Genoa and the Serra Club I had gone to the Holy Father, John XXIII, about a problem existing in the United States at that time. I had been asked to talk over with him a problem that some bishops, notably Cardinal Meyer, were pondering. I was received in audience, as we say. I was a simple bishop, certainly unknown to the Pope! While waiting in the anteroom I felt very worried and kept wondering what form of address I ought to use when speaking to him (you know I don't speak Italian very well!). But I had no chance, as it turned out, of choosing one of the respectful ways of addressing him, for the "Primate" of the Catholic Church began the audience by saying that he, the Pontiff, was happy to make my acquaintance. I was just an ordinary bishop, as I said, and definitely quite unknown to him.

We never got round to the problem about which I had come to Rome. Would you like to know why?

In order to put me at ease, he made a joke. "This name Wright," he said, "is impossible; no one knows how to pronounce it; it only has one vowel, and five consonants! It's like something out of a Russian novel."

He picked up a card from his desk. "Before this Bishop with the strange, almost unpronounceable name arrived, my experts put this here to warn me that, in order to safeguard my dignity, I ought to pronounce your name phonetically, using the sound of the abbreviation for Italian Radio and Television—RAI—and put a T at the end."

"They've given me all kinds of information," he went on, "so that I can know just as much about you as you know about me. That's another way of keeping my dignity. I see you were born in

174

1909; you were at the Gregorian, and you have been secretary—you poor unfortunate—to two archbishops. You have founded a diocese, the name of which is beyond me (Worcester), and were then transferred to the diocese of Pittsburgh. . . . "

I said, "Holiness, you sent me there!".

He looked at the memorandum, saw the date of the transfer, and said, "You're right. So I did. But see what they did to me! I was once Patriarch of Venice! We priests are always being moved about."

He opened a drawer, took another card, and asked, "So you're at Pittsburgh? Is there a college there?".

"There are seven, Holiness," I said.

"Does one of them specialize in technology, a kind of technological institute?"

"Yes, Holiness; it's near where I live. It's called the Carnegie Institute."

"Really? Well, do you know a street called Fair Oaks Avenue?"

"Yes. Two streets from where I live."

"Good," he exclaimed, "there is a certain professor from Venice who is teaching in that Institute. He wants to marry a girl from Venice. She's a teacher too, but in the State of California. This professor saw my Venetian Secretary's name with mine in the newspaper when I was elected Pope, and he has written to me to ask for an Apostolic Blessing for his marriage. My Secretary could have gone into any shop around here and had a parchment sent to America, with the Pope's Blessing on it, and it would have been 'valid and genuine.' Yet when he saw that the Bishop of Pittsburgh was down on the list of audiences for today, he asked me to send a medal personally, and a Blessing, some rosary beads and various little souvenirs. Would you do that for me?"

I answered, "It will be a privilege."

But now came the incredible thing. In his holy simplicity he asked, "Would you invite this young couple to your episcopal palace to give them these gifts in the Pope's name?"

I replied, "Holiness, I haven't any palace, but a fairly comfortable house—actually it's a bit big. But I'll phone the professor as soon as I get back, if you will tell me his name."

The Pope said, "The young lady lives in the State of California."

"Holiness, California is farther from Pittsburgh than Moscow is from Rome!"

"How on earth did they meet each other, then?" he exclaimed.

"Holiness, I don't know. May I mention again that I don't know their names."

"Ah!!! Yes! Well, here are their names and the date they are to be married. Invite them along, give them the Holy Father's gifts, and encourage them! Then, at the right moment, *ask them first whether they have been going to Sunday Mass; then suggest a good confession and lots of prayers before the nuptial Mass"*!

This was Pope John! And this was his secret! With all the problems that came to his desk, with all the anguish felt by Christ's Vicar, with all his preoccupations and concern for all the Churches, and . . . as we know now . . . with all his ailments—at that moment he was thinking *personally* how to encourage *two persons* in the *most personal* and pastoral of ways. For him the center of the world (the whole moral universe) was always the person, starting from the divine person of Jesus the Lord Son of the Living God, center and supreme object of his faith, Jesus living in the Holy Catholic Church, Jesus reflected in every person, in that of the professor, of his future bride, in *my* person, in every *person*.

Pope John once remarked that he agreed with his predecessor Pius XII when he said: "The person is not a mere object or inert member of society. He is rather the subject, the basis and the purpose of every society, and has to be acknowledged and appreciated as such."

Pope John always linked this concept of the person with the person of Jesus, as we must always do. In his discourse on "The Person and Peace," he said: "All the critical questions, all the thorny problems which have been waiting for centuries to be solved, depend on the person of Jesus, as do also the whole of history and the problem of life."

But the *person,* the teacher in the Carnegie Institute, his bride, the Bishop, the Priest, in the presence of Jesus himself, they are never isolated from the Church.

They not only belong to the Church, but in a very deep Catholic sense, they form part of it and through it are linked with Jesus himself. The Church founded by Christ—and we must add, the institutional Church!

He joked, laughed, smiled, but never forgot that he was the supreme pontiff, Head of the Church, Christ's Vicar. Inevitably, like all the Roman Pontiffs—not less than Pope Paul VI—he felt himself to be the guardian of the *institutional* Church, even though he saw himself, as does every Pope, as the Church's servant—*Servus Servorum Dei.* The *person* was not in the least abstract for him, and neither was the Church purely mystical, disincarnated or abstract. It was also a Person Whom one knows and loves, the Church instituted by the Lord Jesus, with the Holy Spirit as its soul, giving it the power to survive the crises of the centuries, even—if you will—those periods of triumphalism, which is nowadays described as a symptom of decline, or those periods of iconoclism, which are not less sick. For him the two basic things were the *human person* and *the Church,* including the institutional Church, as Christ willed and human nature demands.

For Pope John, for Pope Paul, for you—and truth to tell—for Jesus himself, the link between the person and the institutional Church always includes the Priest.

Pope John said, "Once this transcendence of religion above everything else has been guaranteed (Christ did not take part in sports or politics, the Pope once remarked cryptically and in passing), the Pastor, whether he be Pope or country priest, will find that the people will come to him with ever less diffidence and with growing enthusiasm" (E. Balducci, op. cit. p. 189).

The need of the hour is the re-kindled hope that we shall always have priests like Father Serra, like Pope John, like Pope Paul, like Peter and Paul the Apostles, like the best of your own parish priests and their associates. This is why Pope John respected the person and loved the Church. Now we can understand the words of a journalist describing Pope John's return from Ostia on March 24th, 1963. He reported his exclamation: "So much youthfulness—how can they be worried only about the things of this earth?", and went on: "The Pope encouraged them to set their sights high, to the highest aim of all: *the priesthood*" (E. Balducci, op. cit. p. 193).

But, like the collegiality of bishops and the Church's whole life, this priesthood goes back to Peter, the Vicar of Christ. Peter's Successor has been there in every part of the Church's history, not as a juridical entity only but as the theological foundation of all the faith, hope, love and unity which make the Church a community. It is so today—it will always be so. Now we can see how Pope John loved the person, the Church, and Jesus above all from his earliest youth, and, though never dreaming that he should be Pope, loved the papacy too, passionately with peace and obedience.

His former Secretary, Mons. Loris Capovilla tells us in his book, *The Heart and Thought of Pope John,* that the Pope's ideas about the papacy were extremely clear. Here are a few of them.

"The history of the world in the millennium that preceded Christ and in the two millennia that have succeeded him is contained in the two Testaments, which describe the relations between God and mankind.

"In the Old Testament the Lord speaks to his beloved people, to whom he gave the task of preparing the world for the coming of his universal kingdom, the Church.

"The confidant, the recipient and the interpreter of the divine words was a man, the greatest man of ancient history: Moses.

"God's light always shone in him. Everything takes its inspiration from him: the Patriarchs who went before him, the Judges, the Kings, and the Prophets, who followed him. *Moses is the center of the Old Testament.*

"In the New Testament, God resumes his relationship with man, but not with one race only: with all the peoples of the earth—This shows that the mystery of the Chosen People had been entirely revealed. The Lord who often and in various ways spoke to the Fathers in the Old Testament through the Prophets, now sent *his own Son,* Jesus Christ, God made man, in order to speak more clearly and with more majesty.

"God sent him to warn, to prepare the law that would be universal, to proclaim himself the light of the world—the Way, the Truth and the Life—and to seal with his own blood the supreme sacrament of the inward union of the divine with the human. Christ's law is the holy rule of regenerated humanity, the everlasting Good News to be announced to all nations, both present and future.

"Jesus, Son of God and son of Mary, needed only thirty years to complete his mission. But at the time when his life on earth was drawing to its close, he willed that his presence should be extended into the centuries to come through the two mysteries of the Eucharist and the papacy.

"Among his followers was one whom Jesus chose with great care: Simon, son of John. Jesus chose to call him Peter, as if through that one name and the image it suggests he wished to give greater prominence to the mission he would entrust to him. 'And I say to thee, thou art Peter, and upon this rock I will build my Church, and the powers of hell shall not prevail against it. And I will give to thee the keys of the kingdom of heaven, and whatever thou shalt bind upon earth shall be bound also in heaven, and whatever thou shalt loose upon earth shall be loosed also in heaven' (Matthew 16, 18-19). And again, 'Feed my lambs . . . Feed my sheep' (John 21, 15-17).

"Just as in the Old Testament Moses, Aaron's brother, was

179

God's great confidant, Lawgiver and Prophet, so also in the New Testament Peter is Prince of the Apostles, Teacher, Pontiff and Universal Pastor. The world looked on with confidence when the Lord chose Peter. The choice raised Peter above his lowly origins.

"The world received him with love; it admired him and wished to follow him."

Was there perhaps some divine secret in Pope John's pontificate? Yes, there certainly was. But it is also Pope Paul's secret, for it belongs to the papacy itself! It is a special identity with the *person* of Christ.

But, you may well ask what was the problem I had gone to him to discuss. The fact is that it had to do—and he knew it—with the staggering problem of vocations, the finding of new aides to the Pope and images of Christ. I had with me a bundle of sociological surveys, psychological studies, impressive statistics. The truly holy man never got around to them! After ardent promises and requests for prayer, he eased me on my way, sending pledges of prayer and pleas for yet more pastoral work to the worried bishops at home.

"What did the Pope say about our problem?" Cardinal Meyer asked when I phoned him that I was home. I could only reply that he had personally asked me to do a bit of pastoral work with a couple about to marry—and that he said my name was impossible to pronounce!"

"Well, what about our problem and all those reports?" the scholarly American prelate persisted. I could only reply that the Pope clearly thought there was need for much prayer and lots more love of persons.

"Is that supposed to be the solution of this complex problem?" he asked wistfully. "I doubt it," I replied, "but the Pope seemed to think it was the unavoidable beginning."

Appendix

1. "The Church of Promise"
   Address to the Knights of Columbus Convention
   Knights of Columbus Center
   New Haven, Connecticut
   August 20, 1969

2. "Teachers of the Faith"
   Address at the Catechetical Seminar (originally in Italian)
   Passo della Mendola
   Province of Trent
   Northern Italy
   August 9, 1969

3. "Faith and the Theologies"
   Address for the Renewal Course in Theology
   for the Clergy of the Archdiocese of
   Florence, Italy (given in Italian)
   December 28, 1970

4. "The Point of Contemporary Catechetics
   Opening Address to the International Catechetical Congress
   Rome
   September 20, 1971

5. "Christ Head of the Church and the Priest"
   Article written for "Seminarium" a review edited
   by the Congregation for Catholic Education
   Vatican City
   January, 1970

6. "Priestly Maturity"
   Article written for "Seminarium."
   Vatican City
   September 1970

7. "The Resurrection: Fact or Myth?"
   Homily, Church of the Divine Teacher
   Cardinal Wright's Titular Church in Rome
   Easter, 1970
8. "Justice Exalts"
   Homily at the Labor Day Mass
   St. Paul's Cathedral
   Pittsburgh, Pennsylvania
   September 1, 1969
9. "Faith and Social Action"
   Homily, Church of the Divine Teacher
   as Cardinal Wright took possession of
   his titular church
   Rome
   May 2, 1969
10. "The Blessed Vision of Peace"
    Homily, Mass for Peace
    Propaganda Fide College
    Rome
    January 15, 1970
11. "The Cult of Mary in the Age of the Cult of the Flesh"
    Homily, Basilica of Our Lady of Pompei (Italian)
    Pompei, Italy
    December 8, 1969
12. "The Roman Loyalty of the English Martyrs"
    Article for the *L'Osservatore Romano*
    (English Edition)
    October 22, 1971
13. "Toast to the Holy Father"
    The toast delivered at the reunion of the
    North American College Alumni
    Boston, Massachusetts
    May 13, 1970
14. "Pope John and His Secret"
    Address to the Serra Club (Italian)
    Genova, Italy
    December 21, 1969

Index

191